In Search of Pegasus

Dedication

*This book is dedicated to all Canadian
paratroopers, past, present and future, who
have dared answer the call of the Jumpmaster.*

In Search of Pegasus

THE CANADIAN AIRBORNE EXPERIENCE 1942-1999

Bernd Horn & Michel Wyczynski

Vanwell Publishing Limited
St. Catharines, Ontario

Vanwell Publishing Limited
1 Northrup Crescent
P.O. Box 2131
St. Catharines, Ontario L2R 7S2

USA address:
Vanwell Publishing Limited
P.O. Box 1207
Lewiston, NY 14092

Canadian Cataloguing in Publication Data

Horn, Bernd, 1959-
        In search of Pegasus : the Canadian Airborne experience 1942-1999

Includes bibliographical references and index.
ISBN 1-55125-039-X

1. Canada — Armed Forces — Airborne troops — History. I. Wyczynski, Michel, 1953
— .II. Title.

UD485.C3H67 2000   356'.166'0971   C00-932343-0

Printed in Canada

TABLE OF CONTENTS

V

ACKNOWLEDGEMENTS

Any project of this magnitude inherently is indebted to numerous individuals who have contributed their expertise, memories and time. Our deepest gratitude is extended to all those who assisted, either directly or indirectly, in this book. Although it would be impossible to individually acknowledge everyone, the significant contributions of some oblige us to make special mention of their efforts. In this regard, we wish to convey our sincere gratitude to: Tony Balasevicius, Eamonn Barry, Lynn Bullock, Jan de Vries, Fraser Eadie, B.A.J. Franklin, Jacqueline Guimond, Don Halcrow, Stephen Harris, Ron Haycock, Janet Lacroix, Ronson Okerlund, Robert Prouse, Mark Thibodeau and Yves Tremblay. We must also make special mention of the selfless efforts and enormous support of the staff of the National Archives of Canada, the Canadian Forces Photographic Unit Central Negative Library, the Canadian Airborne Forces Museum, the Canadian War Museum, and the Royal Canadian Regiment (RCR), Princess Patricia's Canadian Light Infantry (PPCLI), and Royal 22nd Regiment (R22eR) regimental museums. Notwithstanding the contributions of these aforementioned individuals and institutions, there are two people, without whose constant support and understanding we could not have completed this project. We wish to acknowledge our deepest gratitude to our wives, Kim and Suzanne, who so patiently and tolerantly not only suffered our quest, but actively encouraged and nurtured it. It is to them that we owe our largest debt for the completion of this book

PREFACE

Born from the fires of a global conflict, Canada's first paratroop battalion commenced a legacy of courage, professionalism and tenacity which has been emulated by its heirs ever since. This book tells the paratroopers' story. It is intended as a tribute to the service and achievements of Canada's airborne forces, specifically to those individuals who have perpetually represented the Army's vanguard force, ready to go anywhere, anytime.

Often ignored, if not neglected, and overwhelmingly misunderstood, Canada's airborne soldiers have existed largely on the periphery of the military institution, as well as of society at large. But despite their repeated marginalization, their spirit has always remained undaunted. Undeniably, the nation's paratroopers have consistently represented the best of the country's combat soldiers.

Our book relies heavily on photographs to recount the various eras in the Canadian airborne experience. This was a conscious decision. Words are often inadequate to capture the drama of human endeavour. They cannot always fully capture the human spirit or personal emotion. Words are often misconstrued and open to varied interpretation. Conversely, pictures are snapshots in time. They can capture the soul of their subject and provide a clarity that eludes the most eloquent writer. Accordingly, we decided not to inundate the work with a plethora of documentary endnotes.

Nevertheless, the information in both photograph captions and accompanying text was meticulously researched. We relied almost exclusively on original textual records, photographs and caption logs held by the DND Directorate of History and Heritage, the National Archives of Canada, the Canadian Airborne Forces Museum, and the Canadian Forces Photographic Unit Central Negative Library, as well as the Royal Canadian Regiment (RCR), the Princess Patricia's Canadian Light Infantry (PPCLI), and the Royal 22nd Regiment (R22eR) regimental museums. Our work also brings forward information culled from official war diaries (both unit and Canadian Forces bases), historical reports, as well as other military and governmental documents. Personal interviews were conducted with serving and former serving paratroopers representing every era of the Canadian airborne experience.

However, the human memory is a fickle tool, and great care was taken to ensure consistency with other elements of the historical record. We hope that this dual format will assist in outlining the historical role and operational contribution of the Canadian paratrooper to the Canadian defence effort, both at home and abroad.

As a final note, personal interpretation of material is a critical element of the final presentation of a work of this nature. In this regard, the background of both authors is mutually supportive. Both are serving military members, one in the Regular Force with airborne service, the other in the Reserve, without parachute experience. One author is trained as a military historian, while the other is a professional archivist. Together, our varied military and professional training and expertise have, we hope, brought forward accuracy and balance on this unique historical issue.

FOREWORD

This book represents the first substantial attempt to chronicle the entire Canadian airborne experience, which spans a period of more than fifty-six years.

For much of that time I remained a part of the airborne family. I shall ever remember, with great pride and affection, the energy and spirit of Canada's first paratroopers who forged a proud legacy on the battlefields of Europe during the Second World War.

An unprecedented level of physical fitness, an unrivaled skill-at-arms, and an unparalleled sense of self-confidence characterized the early airborne soldier. These paratroopers became the first Canadian troops to storm Hitler's Fortress Europe on D-Day. By war's end they had penetrated deeper into the Reich than any other Canadian unit. There was never a challenge too great, no task too daunting.

But what struck me over the years was the consistency of this unique airborne spirit. Throughout their brief history, the nature and structure of the country's parachute units has ebbed and flowed. Predictably, the faces and the names of those serving continually changed. Nevertheless, the soul of the innumerable airborne organizations, specifically reflected in the attitude and performance of the individual

LCol G.F. Eadie, Commander of 1 Canadian Parachute Battalion, in Grelingen, Germany, 8 April 1945. *(Lt C.H. Richer, NA, Neg. PA169240)*

Fraser Eadie, Colonel of the Regiment, Canadian Airborne Regiment, 1989-1994. *(Fraser Eadie)*

paratroopers, persistently endured. It always remained: to go a little farther; to move across country a little faster; to be a little more cunning.

Remarkably, the authors have commendably captured the activities and spirit of Canada's airborne soldiers. Their careful research and attention to detail are mirrored in the text and photographs which chronicle the often misunderstood realm of Canada's parachute organizations.

Long overdue, the following pages acknowledge the service and achievements of this nation's airborne forces, particularly of the intrepid individuals who dared answer the Jumpmaster's call.

LCol Fraser Eadie (Ret'd) DSO, CD

PART I

INTRODUCTION

The waging of war from the heavens has been an age-old dream. The mythical Greek hero Bellerophon astride his winged horse Pegasus, was the earliest manifestation of this concept.

The advantage bestowed on an airborne warrior was axiomatically apparent. The potential was so great that Benjamin Franklin, during a visit to Paris in 1784, posed the rhetorical question, "Where is the Prince who can afford so to cover his country with troops for its defence, as that ten thousand men descending from the clouds might not, in many places, do an infinite deal of mischief before a force could be brought together to repel them?"

Two decades later, in 1805, during the ill-fated preparations for Napoleon's planned invasion of England, the notion of using balloons to carry assault troops across the channel was seriously considered. The existence of a special formation, designated the *Compagnie d'Aérostiers*, which had been established on 23 March 1794, provided a solid rationale for this proposal. The *Compagnie* possessed four balloons, each with a permanent assigned crew. French military planners placed such great faith in the potential of this unit that they postulated that 2,500 of these four-man balloons, launched prior to a sea invasion, would cause chaos, if not the complete surrender of the English forces.

This futuristic scheme, however, similar to Napoleon's invasion plans, never came to fruition. The concept of unleashing assault troops from the skies subsequently underwent a lengthy hiatus. The idea next emerged in the shadow of the costly and stagnant battlefields of the First World War.

Colonel William Mitchell, Commander of the United States Army Air Corps in France, was the catalyst behind the next significant advancement in the development of airborne forces. In October 1918, he initiated an innovative scheme designed to overcome the deadlock of trench warfare. He suggested that soldiers of the 1st US Infantry Division (Big Red One) be equipped with individual parachutes and armed with a preponderance of machine guns. He further advanced the idea that this lethal cargo would then be dropped behind enemy lines by his great force of bombardment aircraft. This group of parachute infantry, Mitchell explained, could then "attack the Germans from the rear, aided by an attack from our army on the front." This endeavour, he insisted, would also be supported by the entire American air force in the European theatre.

Remarkably, Mitchell's superiors accepted his daring plan. However, the armistice was implemented unexpectedly prior to the realization of Mitchell's avant-garde thinking.

Surprisingly, his vision did not die. The Italians were the first to demonstrate the sagacity and practical application of Colonel Mitchell's concept. In 1927, they astonished the world by simultaneously dropping nine men and their equipment. Inexplicably, the Italian experimentation soon died out, but the Soviet Union quickly discerned the potential of parachuting and continued to pioneer the theory of airborne warfare. In the process they advanced the idea to unprecedented heights. The Soviets displayed innovation and a grasp for tactics.

The Russian experience in the First World War, as well as during their subsequent civil war, left an indelible mark on the psyche of the new regime. As a direct result, Soviet military planners and strategists quickly seized on the importance of manoeuvre, speed, and sur-

prise. The belief in bold, aggressive action emerged supreme. This new faith inherently dictated the development of a doctrine that embraced the offensive. Accordingly, the use of airborne forces was viewed as an integral element of this program.

Soviet operational thinking began to focus on the idea of a potential "vertical envelopment." This in turn raised the concept of Deep Battle, which forced an enemy to simultaneously fight both to his front and rear.

The first use of air-landed forces was conducted in 1929, when a heavily armed fifteen-man contingent was inserted into Tadzhikistan to repulse an Afghan Basmachi Moslem rebel force. The arrival of the airborne soldiers reportedly broke the siege of the town of Garm.

Marshal Mikhail Tukhachevsky, the Commander of the Leningrad Military District, actively promoted further Soviet experimentation. Tukhachevsky envisioned joint, as well as combined-arms offensive operations. He stressed the coordinated utilization of motorized rifle units, self-propelled artillery, and aviation to crack the enemy's outer defences. To support the main effort, Tukhachevsky proposed the use of bombers to interdict enemy reserves. But, more importantly, he asserted that a new genre of warriors, namely paratroopers, would be used to seize vital targets and block an enemy's withdrawal. Their utilization, he insisted, would allow "a crushing blow to be delivered by the second echelon of forces."

Tukhachevsky began to conduct trial airborne exercises in 1929. By the summer of 1933, the official Soviet military publication, *Temporary Instructions on the Combat Use of Aviation Landing Units*, emphasized the requirement for airborne forces to engage in bold manoeuvres to capitalize on the element of surprise and to effect the speedy employment and rapid concentration of force.

Significantly, all Soviet field exercises from 1933 onwards included airborne operations. Two years later, manoeuvres in the Kiev region demonstrated the Soviet capability of simultaneously dropping more than one thousand parachutists. This stunning military feat was witnessed by numerous military attachés. Although they were impressed by the spectacle, no real interest was galvanized. Major-General Archibald Wavell, the British attaché, commented, "This Parachute descent, though its tactical value may be doubtful, was a most spectacular performance."

But the Soviets were far more persistent. By 1936, they had conceptually refined their idea of Deep Battle. Moreover, they validated their theory by implementation during field exercises. Furthermore, their ideas were now entrenched in their operational doctrine. "Major units of parachute forces," stated the Red Army Field Regulations, "provide an effective means of disrupting the enemy's command, control and logistics. In conjunction with frontal attack, they may play a decisive part in achieving complete destruction of the enemy on a given axis."

Incredibly, the Soviet developments were quickly lost in the turmoil of the Stalinist purges which eliminated the supporters of the concept of airborne warfare. Their replacements failed to understand the value of the newly developed airborne forces. As a result, the concept of Deep Battle slowly dissipated.

The momentum gained, however, was not entirely lost. The Germans carefully studied and analyzed the Russian airborne advancements. Moreover, they expanded and improved the theory and practise of airborne operations. The Germans quickly undertook the practical application of parachuting for internal security operations. Polizeimajor Hans Wecke, of the Prussian Police Force, utilized a small task force which parachuted into suspected communist hideouts. The shock and surprise effect of his small force was exceedingly successful, and it was later absorbed into the Luftwaffe.

The German effort at building an airborne capability progressed rapidly. In the autumn of 1935, the Luftwaffe Chief of Staff, General Walther Wever, successfully persuaded Reichsmarschall Hermann Göring that the newly formed Hermann Göring Regiment should be trained as parachutists. This led to the establishment of the first German parachute battalion and provided the catalyst for the creation of a parachute school in Stendal a year later.

After the death of General Wever, General Kurt Student took up the airborne cause which Wever in many respects had pioneered. Undeniably, Student became the pre-eminent champion of the German air-

borne cause and, as a result, quickly became popularly recognized as the father of the German parachute forces. Student clearly understood the value of his Fallschirmjägers (paratroops). "Airborne troops," he asserted, "could become a battle-winning factor of prime importance." Student declared that "airborne forces made third-dimensional warfare possible in land operations. An adversary could never be sure of a stable front because paratroops could simply jump in and attack it from the rear where and when they decided."

He emphasized the effect of the psychological shock that a sudden attack from the sky would produce on an adversary. Paratroopers, he explained, could "pounce down and take over before the foe knows what is going on." Student insisted that "the element of surprise and shock action of paratroopers dropping in what was considered a safe area instilled panic in the defender prior to the first shot being fired."

The Germans conducted the first small airborne exercise in 1937. By the next year the airborne forces were expanded to create the 7th Flieger Division which grouped both Luftwaffe and Wehrmacht parachutists. The first mass drop of German paratroops occurred on 7 October 1938. This event prompted Reichsmarschall Göring to comment, "This weapon has a great future."

Parallel airborne developments in the other major powers were virtually non-existent. The French had limited their foray into airborne warfare with the establishment in 1938 of only two airborne companies. These were subsequently disbanded when the war began. The Americans and the British were even less interested. Both of these international powers saw limited utility in the use of airborne forces.

In 1939 General G.E. Lynch, Chief of Infantry in Washington, conducted a study on the uses of "air infantry" for the American army's Chief of Staff. The resultant report affirmed little faith in the ability to achieve a large victory by use of airborne forces. It rated paratroopers as having limited potential and opted for an unimaginative recommendation of further study and lengthy experimentation to determine composition and size of possible units.

Global events, however, shattered the existing lethargy. The daring German airborne operations in Norway and the Low Countries in the spring of 1940 quickly converted the non-believers. The German aerial onslaught became the catalyst for action. By 6 June 1940, British Prime Minister Winston Churchill began to assail his staff with proposals to develop a corps of parachute troops. Several weeks later he sent a memorandum to the Chiefs of Staff urging them to establish a corps of at least five thousand parachute troops. To Churchill, the offensive was all that mattered, and paratroopers undeniably encapsulated the warrior spirit so close to his heart. Accordingly, the combative British prime minister became the stimulus for the establishment of airborne forces in the British army.

However, it was not an easy task. The vehement resistance from his military commanders necessitated his continual prodding for progress reports to ensure headway was being made. Lieutenant-General F.A.M. Browning, also a strong advocate for paratroopers recalled, "very early we came to certain definite conclusions which we have kept before us ever since and for which we may rightly say we have fought many a stout battle against the doubters and unbelievers: it is always the same with anything new and there is nothing curious about that." The enmity was initially so entrenched that it prompted Churchill to suggest to Anthony Eden, the British Secretary of State for War, that an example should be made of "one or two" of the reluctant officers so the others would better follow political direction.

The events in Europe also prompted the Americans to accelerate their airborne program. Nevertheless, as for their English brethren, conservatism was the watchword. On 26 June 1940, the Americans created a "test platoon." This meagre effort, however, was soon eclipsed when the Axis war machine once again galvanized the Allied effort. The German capture of the Mediterranean island of Crete, primarily by airborne forces, in May 1941 provided the final push. Henceforth, as the Germans de-emphasized the role of their paratroopers due to the heavy casualties the seizure of Crete entailed, the Allies embarked upon an unprecedented build-up of airborne forces.

PART II
BEGINNINGS

THE ESTABLISHMENT OF
A CANADIAN AIRBORNE
CAPABILITY, 1942-1945

anada, much like the United States and Britain during the interwar years, expended little to no thought on the concept of airborne forces. There were no military initiatives taken to examine or even consider the impact of paratroopers on modern warfare. Nor was there even debate in the Canadian Defence Quarterly on this issue, such as was raging on the topic of mechanization. As a result, when the German Blitzkrieg struck the Low Countries and France, the Canadian military, much like their allies, were mesmerized by the seeming invincibility of the German Fallschirmjägers.

Overnight, Europe was gripped by an airborne paranoia. The spectre of airborne soldiers descending into hitherto safe regions even extended across the Channel to England. Even the spirited and offensive-minded Prime Minister Winston Churchill expected a German invasion of Britain spearheaded by thirty thousand German paratroops.

The parachute scare touched the Canadian overseas contingent as well. The expeditious withdrawal from the European continent under the pressure of the German juggernaut left an indelible imprint on the

"Picked men from Canada's Army overseas." These Canadian soldiers have just completed their basic parachutist course (12 September 1942) in RAF Parachute School, Ringway in Cheshire, England. Subsequently they proceeded to Fort Benning, Georgia to form the nucleus of the First Canadian Parachute Battalion.

(Capt Frank Royal, NAC, PA204956)

Calling the jump manifest. Paratroopers prepare for a training jump in Fort Benning, in the fall of 1942.

(1 Cdn Para Bn Assn, donated by N. Wilton)

Canadian military personnel involved in that brief sojourn. Now in England and charged with the defence of the island, the need to defend against the airborne threat was a preeminent concern.

Amazingly, despite the apparent success and potential of parachute forces, the Canadian military command gave no consideration to the concept of paratroopers other than how to defend against them. This short-sighted approach, however, was rejected by Colonel E.L.M. Burns. He witnessed first-hand the effectiveness of the German Blitzkrieg in Europe in the spring of 1940. He also felt the full effect of the parachute scare in Britain following the retreat from the mainland. Colonel Burns, renowned for his intellect and prolific writing on mechanization during the interwar years, immediately recognized the strategic value of the new airborne forces. To Burns they exemplified a means of striking the enemy's command and logistical facilities behind the front lines, thus paralyzing a belligerent's front-line combat forces. Paratroops, much like the "motor guerillas" expounded by the famous British military theorist, J.F.C. Fuller, now opened the possibility of a new operational dimension. Distance was no longer a factor. Paratroopers, Burns realized, made the concept of a safe rear area obsolete.

In July 1940, Burns returned to Canada to fulfill the appointment as the Assistant Deputy to the Chief of the General Staff. Burns was personally selected by Major-General H.D.G. Crerar, the newly appointed Chief of the General Staff (CGS), specifically to undertake the monumental job of organizing and developing the Canadian Army to meet the formidable task which lay ahead.

Fresh from his experiences overseas, Burns immediately attempted to create a distinct parachute force for the Army. On 13 August 1940, a mere two months after his arrival in Canada, Burns submitted a proposal to Colonel J.C. Murchie, Director of Military Operations, National Defence Headquarters (NDHQ), recommending the establishment of a Canadian parachute capability. Murchie was unreceptive to the arguments brought forward by Burns, and saw no value in raising and training such troops as part of Canada's war effort. Murchie believed that paratroopers, in view of the time, money, and equipment involved, were prohibitively expensive in resources, particularly at this critical juncture of the war. Of equal concern was the realization that these troops, because of the small numbers Canada could provide, as well as the operational role they would perform, would most likely be placed under British command. The issue of national command, which had been so hard fought for in the First World War, was a very formidable concern.

Nevertheless, Burns remained undeterred. Armed with Murchie's observations and criticisms, Colonel Burns submitted a second memorandum directly to the Chief of the General Staff, Major-General Crerar. Colonel Burns now took a slightly different tack. He argued for a parachute capability in an exclusively Canadian context. Colonel Burns explained that raising parachute troops would be an efficient means of countering enemy raids and attacks on Canadian soil. The paratroopers, he argued, could provide rapid deployment to remote parts of Canada's coastline, which could not be reached quickly by conventional troops.

Crerar appeared to be receptive to the report but felt that "it was not a project of importance to the winning of the war just now." However, Crerar directed Burns to bring the issue to his attention in three months' time. On 12 November 1940, Colonel Burns submitted his third and final memorandum to the CGS. In his latest effort, Burns emphasized the success of the German Fallschirmjägers, as well as ongoing American and British initiatives concerning the establishment and training of airborne forces. Burns also stressed that parachute troops had become a key proponent of a modern army, and as such he projected that one day the Allies would be on the offensive and would require such troops to operate behind enemy lines to force the Germans to establish and maintain larger rear-echelon defence garrisons. This, he explained, would minimize the number of combat troops available to oppose the inevitable Allied invasion of Festung Europa.

Burns also realized the propaganda value of a parachute-training program. He felt that the possession of paratroopers would stimulate public and military morale. "It would be a step toward a 'quality' army," he stated, "and would show that we were actually doing something to create a force with offensive capabilities." Burns's latest effort generated some discussion within NDHQ but, as

Cpl N. R. Chapman trains on the high tower shock harness.   *(Harry Rowed, NA, PA205024)*

before, the senior military leadership failed to see the relevance of a national parachute capability. As a result, nothing was done. Moreover, by the spring of 1941, Colonel Burns was promoted and returned to duty overseas.

With the departure of Burns, the undisputed champion of the Canadian airborne cause to date, the issue of raising parachute troops underwent a lengthy hiatus. Nevertheless, the idea of Canadian paratroops continued to smolder. The issue was occasionally re-examined by senior military officers in NDHQ and in the Canadian Military Headquarters in London (CMHQ). Remarkably, the catalyst was the continual prodding of the Royal Canadian Air Force, who persistently requested the Army's position on the establishment of airborne forces. The RCAF commanders understood that paratroopers represented a requirement for more aircraft and an expanded role for the air force.

Nonetheless, the Army maintained a consistent response. Each time, they enunciated the same conclusion, namely, that there was no operational role or mandate for such a unit in the current structure of the Canadian Army.

In spring 1942, this point was hammered home by none other than James Layton Ralston, the Minister of National Defence. "The formation of paratroop units," he announced to Parliament on 22 April 1942, "is not being gone ahead with at the present moment, but rather the training of men so they can be used as paratroopers when the time comes, with additional training to be done with aircraft." Despite this qualified declaration, which had been used as early as December 1940 by the CGS, the truth was that no such training had been undertaken or was in the process of commencing.

Distinctive landmarks, three of the four high towers in Fort Benning, March 1943.
(Lt S.E. Smith, NA, PA204980)

Controlled descents on the high tower.
(Harry Rowed, NA, PA205018)

Fort Benning's parachute training apparatus, including mock towers and dummy aircraft fuselages, are used to practise aircraft drills and exits.
(1 Cdn Para Bn Assn, donated by D.R. Fairborn)

Practising "flight" drills in Fort Benning. *(Lt S.E. Smith, NA, PA204979)*

Mock tower in Fort Benning. *(Lt S.E. Smith, NA, PA204978)*

Paradoxically, as the defence minister attempted to put an end to the debate on paratroop units, the Army was beginning to reconsider its position. The genesis of this new interest lay in the efforts of its two closest allies. The German seizure of Crete in May 1941 finally galvanized the American and British interests in airborne forces. Both adopted the belief that paratroopers epitomized the offensive, and were in fact pivotal in modern warfare. Concomitant with this belief was the rapid build-up of American and British airborne forces. Both of Canada's allies were now creating airborne divisions.

Not to be left out, senior Canadian military commanders now revisited the question of a parachute unit. The Directorate of Military Training at NDHQ carefully examined the parachute training that was being conducted by its two allies. In June, the director dispatched Lieutenant-Colonel R.H. Keefler to the US Army Parachute School in Fort Benning, Georgia, to assess their training methods, techniques and facilities. Keefler's report as well as the observations and recommendations of Air Vice Marshal Steadman of the RCAF, who had just returned from a visit with the 6th (UK) Airborne Division, now seemed to propel the idea of a national airborne capability beyond the doctrinal and psychological barrier behind which it had stalled for so many years.

In light of the new emphasis the Allies placed on paratroops, and the improving war situation, Major-General Murchie reassessed his position with regard to the establishment of Canadian airborne forces. Murchie now forwarded a proposal to the Minister of National Defence recommending the organization of a parachute battalion.

Remarkably, the new attitude was quickly embraced by both the senior Canadian military and political leadership.

On 1 July 1942 the War Cabinet Committee approved the establishment of a parachute battalion. However, the committee asserted that the purpose of this unit was home defence, specifically the recapture of aerodromes or reinforcement of remote localities.

Ironically, the inconsistency of the entire issue seemed to be ignored. During the early years of the war, when the shadow of German victory was greatest, the relevance and utility of paratroopers for use in the defence of Canada, with its large expanses of unprotected shorelines and territory, was discounted. Yet, as the tide of the war shifted and the potential threat to Canada all but disappeared, the senior leaders decided to create a parachute force for defensive purposes. However, as events would reveal, the paratroopers' role was not to be defensive in nature. Messages were quickly sent to all Military Districts calling for volunteers to become paratroopers. Concurrently, and as an interim measure, NDHQ submitted a request to the American authorities to send candidates to Fort Benning for parachute training. American approval provided the ability to quickly commence training for the volunteers, as well as to conduct further research as to the type of training facilities and special equipment required to set up a separate Canadian parachute training centre. On 25 July, an Inter-Service Committee selected Camp Shilo, Manitoba, as the site for the parachute-training centre. It was now only a question of time to erect the necessary facilities to support the training.

As the efforts to prepare Shilo commenced, the first group of twenty-seven volunteers for parachute training assembled in Lansdowne Park, Ottawa, in mid August 1942, under the command of Major H. D. Proctor. This intrepid group subsequently deployed to Fort Benning, Georgia, to commence their American parachute training. Simultaneously, a second contingent of ninety-six candidates was selected from Canadian troops stationed in England. This group was sent to the Parachute Training School, Royal Air Force Station Ringway, in Cheshire, England. They, in turn, trained in accordance with British parachute methods. Although the Canadian airborne program had had a slow start, it now attempted to make up for lost time.

The parachute training in Fort Benning was marred by the tragic death of Major Proctor during his first jump on 7 September 1942. His death, along with the demanding training regimen, quickly instilled in the aspiring paratroopers the physical and psychological demands of this new type of warfare. Their personal courage and motivation were tested every time they stepped up to the door to jump.

It also quickly became evident that not everyone was capable of becoming a paratrooper. Many would volunteer,

Parachute candidates with their American Jumpmaster.

"Check your equipment!" The jumpmaster conducts his final check before dispatching this "stick" of paratroopers during a training jump in Fort Benning.

Parachute training in Fort Benning. The early American instruction on landing technique stressed the importance of maintaining the feet apart at shoulder width and executing a forward roll upon contact with the earth. Conversely, the British method emphasized keeping the feet and knees together. Upon landing the paratroopers were taught to conduct a side-roll, ensuring that body contact with the ground followed a sequence of feet, knees and shoulders. Not surprisingly, the American method entailed a higher casualty rate.

(Ken Bell, Canadian Forces Photographic Unit Central Negative Library (CFPU CNL), ZK-158)

The dangers of a crowded sky. Two paratroopers require assistance to get themselves untangled on the DZ / "Frying Pan" of Fort Benning, fall 1942.

(Ken Bell, CFPU CNL, ZK-163)

but only a few would earn the coveted jump wings. On average only 30 percent passed the initial screening process. Of these successful candidates another 30 to35 percent would be lost as training failures and returned to their respective units.

Notwithstanding the high wastage rate, the Canadian airborne program forged ahead. The initial two groups of paratroopers that were sent for training to Fort Benning and Ringway were assembled at the termination of their respective courses at Fort Benning. This cadre was debriefed, and a distinct Canadian parachute training program was then drafted encompassing the best of the American and British parachute techniques, to take effect once the Canadian parachute training centre was ready to open.

But no delay was tolerated. Training for the new paratroop unit was to begin as quickly as possible. In late September 1942, Lieutenant-Colonel G.F.P. Bradbrooke was appointed Commanding Officer of the 1 Canadian Parachute Battalion (1 Cdn Para Bn). He was immediately immersed in the myriad of administrative and operational problems, such as recruiting, locating and ordering the required equipment and weaponry, and preparing a challenging training syllabus.

The establishment of a new unit is never without frustration and a certain degree of growing pains. Bradbrooke knew the importance of instilling an esprit de corps and looked into various items of dress that could assist in developing a sense of belonging and unit pride, and that would ultimately forge a unique Canadian airborne identity. Maintaining morale and unit efficiency became increasing difficult because Bradbrooke was not only plagued with equipment deficiencies, he quickly faced a more serious dilemma-retaining his qualified jumpers. A second parachute unit, designated the 2 Canadian Parachute Battalion (2 Cdn Para Bn) had been established in July.

This unit title, however, was misleading. It was not a parachute battalion, but rather a commando unit. The designation was merely given for security reasons to cover the true operational mandate of its members. This unit was later re-designated the First Canadian Special Service Force Battalion on 25 May 1943. It represented the Canadian element of the joint US/Canadian First Special Service Force (FSSF). Its immediate priority on resources, including manpower, created a grave problem for 1 Cdn Para Bn. NDHQ directed Bradbrooke to transfer all jump-qualified personnel who volunteered to 2 Cdn Para Bn. Rumour quickly circulated throughout the ranks of 1 Cdn Para Bn that this new unit would see action in the very near future. Not surprisingly, many of the aggressive and action-seeking paratroopers became frustrated with their Battalion's seemingly slow activation and transferred to 2 Cdn Para Bn.

To make matters worse morale deteriorated even further during the fall of 1942, when senior military leadership directed that National Resources Mobilization Act (NRMA) personnel were entitled to join 1 Cdn Para Bn. The paratroopers were incensed. This implied that the Battalion would never see active duty overseas since the NRMA personnel were designated for Home Defence service only. Those responsible for the establishment of the new parachute unit quickly advised the CGS that the wrong type of candidate was being sent to the battalion and that this in turn was causing serious recruiting and retention problems. The CGS expeditiously rectified this situation by announcing that "all parachute volunteers for the 1 Cdn Para Bn must be active personnel."

"Home Defence personnel," he explained, "were to be accepted only if they 'went active' prior to their dispatch from their home district."

With one more problem overcome, another presented itself. The Battalion's anticipated relocation to Camp Shilo was deferred until March 1943. An agreement to provide facilities to the US Army for cold-weather testing had created a shortage of space. Priorities of the day necessitated that the paratroopers be bumped.

To add further misery, ninety-seven paratroopers volunteered for and were subsequently transferred to 2 Cdn Para Bn during the first week in December. Not surprisingly, morale was at a low ebb.

The priority of the new paratroop unit was questioned. The Battalion's War Diary captured the growing frustration. "It is the hope of everyone attached to 1 Cdn Para Bn," the War Diary revealed, "that a clarification of policies, relative to this unit will soon be established by NDHQ. After this Battalion was called up to reinforce the 2nd battalion, the personnel began to feel as though they were lost souls of a lost Battalion."

The 31 December entry, however, closed on a positive note. "We feel confident," it stated, "that the new year will see fulfilment of the original NDHQ plans and the Battalion will be distinguished when called into active combat overseas."

The prophetic words seemed to work. The unit began to form a cohesiveness that subsequent calls for transfers to the First Special Service Force could not break. In addition, challenging training and a steady influx of equipment began to build a distinct sense of confidence and unit pride. The paratroopers of 1 Cdn Para Bn were now growing impatient. They wanted to be tested in battle.

The eagerness to see action was not surprising. The development of an esprit de corps and the emergence of an unprecedented competitive spirit was quickly evident in the mindframe of the young Canadian paratroopers. "The average young parachutists upon graduation from the four-week course in the US Parachute School," noted the Battalion's war diary, "can be aptly described as a 'Bull in a China Shop.'" The entry added that "the psychological transformation of the mind of the most introvert to the extrovert is apparent in most of our young chutists after completing their qualifying jumps and course of Judo. They become fearless and to a degree reckless. They feel as though they have been given the key to all physical success and conquered all phases of fear. It seems to be a trademark of American trained parachute troops to highly estimate their prowess, because of the type of training received, and our Canadian parachutists have acquired a similar frame of mind. This spirit should forge a well knit, hard-hitting force. We members of the 1st Canadian Para Bn, are well aware of our unique position as a newly born unit in a new phase of warfare. We are therefore, confident of the success and trust that we will be given the opportunity to prove our value."

By the spring of 1943, Lieutenant-Colonel Bradbrooke, the Commanding Officer, articulated his understanding of the role he and his soldiers were to play. "The paratroopers," he explained, "are the tip of the spear. They must expect to go in first, to penetrate behind enemy lines and to fight in isolated positions." The training was tailored to prepare the paratroopers for their ordeal of battle. Their reputation for toughness and courage quickly forged a distinct identity in the Army. Understandably, the new jump wings, which were dearly earned and worn with pride by the airborne soldiers, took on a significance that was quickly understood by all.

The paratroopers reported to Camp Shilo, Manitoba, their new home, on 15 April 1943. The tempo of activity in Shilo quickly increased. Bradbrooke's priority was the implementation of a new training schedule for his 621 paratroopers to prepare them for overseas duty. Bradbrooke's focus was simple. It consisted of infantry battle-drills, weapons handling, parachute training, and physical fitness. Route marches became a dreaded component of the training plan. Demanding and gruelling training, which stressed psychological as well as physical strength, conferred on the paratroopers a sense that they were becoming different from the other members of the Canadian Army. Unlike the infantry, the airborne soldiers would have to operate on their own, often behind enemy lines with no secure rear area. The paratroopers would have to rely on their physical fitness, marksmanship, stealth and tenacity to hold their ground until the main force could link up.

While 1 Cdn Para Bn was training at Shilo, Lieutenant-Colonel R.F. Routh, the commanding officer of the new S-14 Canadian Parachute Training School, was preparing his staff to train the first candidates to be jump qualified on Canadian soil. While the training progressed at a rapid pace, the senior leadership attempted to rationalize the employment of the newly formed parachute unit.

Even before the paratroopers were considered operational-ready, they were proffered up to the commander of Home Forces in England. As a result, in March 1943, the British quickly welcomed the offer and stated that 1 Cdn Para Bn would be included in the establishment of the second British airborne division. Despite the immediate deployment overseas and the aggressive spirit of the paratroopers, the Battalion was not yet ready for combat. It had not undergone collective training and would require a further two months of preparation before being fully operational.

Reinforcements required to bring the Battalion up to strength were continually arriving from the now renamed A-35 Canadian Parachute Training Centre. The

Top; Upon arrival at Fort William Henry Harrison Canadian members of the FSSF, after only forty-eight hours of training, conducted their first parachute descent. Their second and final jump occurred the next day. (*US Signal Corps, NA, PA183755*); center from left; A questionable future. The A-35 Canadian Parachute Training Centre's relevance was consistently questioned by Canadian Military Headquarters in London, England. They felt greater efficiency could be realized by sending trainees direct to Fort Benning or Ringway instead of first qualifying them in Shilo and then passing them on for conversion training in Britain. (*1 Cdn Para Bn Assn, donated by Sid Carignan*); The CGS, Lieutenant-General K. Stuart addresses the first class of thirty-three candidates to graduate from the S-14 Canadian Parachute Training School, 13 September 1943, Shilo, Manitoba. The instructional cadre are wearing maroon berets, "Airborne Canada" shoulder titles, Ex Coelis collar badges and Canadian Parachute qualification badges. Candidates are wearing forage caps. (*PPCLI Archives*); Physical fitness training, Rivers, Manitoba. (*1 Cdn Para Bn Assn, donated by Jack Sykes*); Bottom: Parachute candidates dressed for a training jump in Shilo. (*1 Cdn Para Bn Assn, donated by G. Markewich*).

Private Gord McKeown provides an excellent portrait of Canada's early paratrooper training in Fort Benning. He is wearing Canadian battledress, a British jump helmet and Sten gun, and a reserve parachute, which is a departure from the British practise.

(Ken Bell, CFPU CNL, ZK-226)

Canadian paratrooper Lt T.W.R. Brier, wearing an American uniform and highly polished "jump boots" in Fort Benning, fall 1942.

(Ken Bell, CFPU CNL, ZK-356)

specialized training requirement in regard to a paratroop unit quickly became evident. As a result the recommendation to establish a parachute training company, with the specific mandate to train and provide qualified paratroopers as reinforcements for 1 Cdn Para Bn, was implemented.

All the while 1 Cdn Para Bn placed an ever increasing emphasis on training. Time was of the essence. The British airborne division to which the Battalion was to be attached was scheduled to begin its training by June 1943. Moreover, CMHQ learned that the British intended to utilize the Canadian paratroopers for the upcoming operations in North Africa. However, the Canadians quickly stymied this initiative. Military commanders at both NDHQ and CMHQ clearly enunciated that the 1 Cdn Para Bn was intended for operations only in Europe. With the immediate hurdles overcome, the 31 officers and 548 other ranks of 1 Cdn Para Bn deployed from Halifax on board the Queen Elizabeth in late June 1943 for overseas duty.

The paratroopers subsequently disembarked at Greenock, Scotland on 28 July. On arrival, Lieutenant-Colonel Bradbrooke learned that the Battalion would be attached to the 3 Parachute Brigade under the command of Brigadier James Hill, as part of the 6th UK Airborne Division.

The Battalion rapidly settled into their quarters at Carter Barracks at Bulford, Camp Wiltshire and training began in earnest once again. Due to the gruelling nature of airborne warfare, Brigadier James Hill believed that the operational efficiency and survival of his paratroopers depended to a great extent on their fitness. He expected a unit to cover fifty miles in eighteen hours with each soldier carrying a sixty-pound rucksack and weapon. Ten-mile marches within a two-hour time period were also considered the norm. In addition to the necessity for personal fitness, Brigadier Hill based his training philosophy on a few core principles. Control at all times and regardless of circumstances, maximum use of fire effect, simplicity of plan, and speed of thought and action, asserted Hill, were the keys to success.

In sum, the initial two months of training in England were focussed on fitness, weapons handling, and specialist training. The next phase, which lasted until December 1943, concentrated on collective training at battalion and brigade level, particularly operations at night. The Battalion travelled to the bombed-out areas of London and Southampton and conducted live-fire exercises which stressed house-to-house fighting. Throughout this time, a continuing emphasis was still placed on physical fitness and weapons proficiency. Airborne forces are limited by both the types and amounts of weaponry they are able to carry. As a result, maximum effect must be made of each round of ammunition and each respective weapon system. The Battalion also underwent familiarization training on British parachuting techniques and equipment.

The last phase of training, which continued up until the invasion of France, was centred on divisional level activities. This final stage of training was intended to prepare the formation for the upcoming return to the continent. The Battalion continued to excel, prompting Brigadier Hill to comment on their performance during a simulated invasion in early February 1944, "I feel I must write and congratulate you on the excellent show your battalion put up from the Albemarles on Exercise 'Co-operation.' If they continue to make progress in this connection at this rate, they will soon be the best jumping exponents in our airborne corps and I should very much like to see them achieve this end for themselves. Well done."

The paratroopers realized that the moment to storm Hitler's Festung Europa was fast approaching. The preparations and planning for Neptune, the code name for the assault phase of Operation Overlord, the invasion of Europe, were now in their finale stages. The 6th UK Airborne Division headquarters was responsible for protecting the left flank of the 3rd British Infantry Division, which was to land on a beach west of Ouistreham. For the invasion of Europe, the 3 Parachute Brigade was given the daunting tasks of destroying the coastal defence battery at Merville, demolishing the bridges over the River Dives in the areas of Cabourg and Troarn, as well as controlling the high ridge centred on the small village of Le Mesnil. This ridge dominated the landing beaches. Furthermore, the small village of Le Mesnil was a vital crossroads on the Cabourg-Caen highway and thus critical for German efforts to manoeuvre in response to the invasion.

The brigade also had the additional responsibility of harassing and disrupting the German lines of communication and defensive efforts to the greatest extent possible. Brigadier Hill in turn assigned 1 Cdn Para Bn the responsibility of covering the left flank of the 3 Para Brigade's drop zone (DZ) and protecting the brigade's movements within the DZ. In addition, the Battalion was also given three primary missions to be carried out in the eastern and central areas of the Robehomme-Varaville-Le Mesnil sector. A Company was responsible for the defence and protection of the left flank of 9 Para Bn in its approach, march, and attack on the Merville battery. B Company and one section of the Parachute Engineer Squadron were tasked to blow up two bridges spanning the River Dives. C Company, following its pathfinder assignment, was given the supplementary mission of destroying a German headquarters and bridge, as well as neutralizing enemy positions at Varaville.

At 2230 hours, on 5 June 1944, members of C Company, 1 Cdn Para Bn emplaned in Albemarles and left from Harwell Airfield to commence the assault against Hitler's Fortress Europe. These paratroopers were part of the invasion Pathfinder element tasked to secure and prepare the DZs for the main airborne assault. The remainder of the Battalion proceeded to Down Ampney and emplaned in Douglas C-47 aircraft.

The Battalion was airborne by 2300 hours, and so Canada's first paratroopers were about to commence what would become a proud legacy. The Battalion crossed the Channel and dropped into France between 0100 hours and 0130 hours, 6 June 1944. The lack of navigational aids, compounded by the dust and smoke which drifted over the drop zones from the heavy bombing of nearby targets, in addition to enemy anti-aircraft fire, magnified the difficulty of delivering the paratroopers accurately onto their objectives. As a result, the Battalion was scattered over a wide area. On the first drop, only 30 of a possible 110 paratroopers of C Company had landed on the drop zone. The pilots had experienced difficulties recognizing the drop zone's land features, and the navigational systems used proved inefficient. On the second drop the paratroopers of the main airborne group had been scattered over an area forty times greater than planned. One stick was dropped five miles from the drop zone and numerous isolated paratroopers were captured. Elements of B Company landed in marshy terrain which slowed down their advance considerably. In addition, during this drop numerous weapons bags ripped open, scattering the Battalion's much-needed heavy machine guns, mortars, and anti-tank weapons. This significantly reduced the paratroopers' firepower during the following days. These unexpected situations only added to the challenge. By the end of the day, the resiliency of the Canadian paratroopers enabled them to attain all their assigned objectives with less than 30 percent of the troops and equipment originally assigned to the task.

Success, however, was achieved at a great cost. Of the 443 paratroopers that had jumped on 6 June 1944, the Battalion's casualties totalled twenty-one killed or died of wounds, nine wounded, and eighty-six prisoners of war. The remaining paratroopers grimly dug-in to await the inevitable German counterattacks. During the next ten days, 1 Cdn Para Bn secured and defended the Le Mesnil crossroads. Throughout, the dangerously depleted Battalion was instrumental in countering numerous German infantry and armour attacks and mounting reconnaissance patrols to provide information on enemy activities and dispositions. The Canadian paratroopers were briefly pulled from the line for rest and recuperation, but, just as quickly, they were once again returned to their defensive positions at Le Mesnil. This critical piece of real estate was now under constant German artillery and mortar fire. Despite increasing losses, the paratroopers continued their daily combat and reconnaissance patrols and fought off the persistent German counterattacks.

The situation at Le Mesnil slowly evolved into a stalemate. The Battalion was once again pulled from the front and rested during the period from 4 to 20 July. During that time, one hundred non-parachute-qualified infantrymen were sent to reinforce 1 Cdn Para Bn. Following the rest and refit, the unit deployed into the thickly wooded area of Bois de Bavent, south of Le Mesnil. The paratroopers participated in a series of defensive operations and conducted numerous patrols, both by day and night, to identify and locate German positions.

The enemy forces were finally beginning to crumble due to the Allied pressure and as a result, the Germans

Clockwise from top left; 1 Cdn Para Bn officers on board the Queen Elizabeth en route to UK, 26 July 1943. (*Lt C.E. Nye, NA, PA205353*); The Minister of Defence, J.L. Ralston inspects the newly arrived Canadian paratroopers at No. 1 Canadian Base Staging Camp at Chobham, Surrey, 3 August 1943. (*Laurie A. Audrain, NA, PA205354*); Brigadier James Hill talks to (left to right) Capt R.A. MacDonald and Maj P.R. Griffin, British airborne officer, and Maj J.A. Nicklin, Bulford, England, 4 December 1943. (*Sgt E.R. Bonter, NA, PA179678*); British paratroopers exiting a "Whitley" aircraft. (*Photographer unknown, NA, PA205028*)

began selectively to abandon defensive positions. The tide had turned and the Canadian paratroopers were now on the move. For the first time since the Normandy drop, 3 Para Brigade was back on the offensive.

Operation Paddle was launched on 16 August with the object of maintaining contact and pressure on the retreating enemy. The lightly armed paratroopers were ordered not to engage the enemy. Without any armour support they could not counter heavily armed enemy troops or strongholds. Nonetheless, they could identify withdrawal routes, harry their rear guards, and destroy small isolated pockets of resistance.

During the first phase of the operation the Canadian paratroopers were held in reserve. However, the next day the Battalion was returned to the fray. The advance ground to a halt at the St. Samson-Dives sur Mer Canal. The enemy had destroyed the main bridge and it fell to the Canadian paratroopers to locate, capture, and assess the state of four other bridges in the Dives area.

On 18 August, at 2145 hours, the Battalion commenced operations. A little more than two hours later it had captured the four bridges and 150 prisoners and destroyed approximately two enemy companies and their heavily fortified defensive positions.

After the four bridges were secured, 1 Cdn Para Bn was designated the vanguard unit and the advance was continued. Drawing heavy fire from the retreating German troops, the paratroopers pushed on and captured the towns of Annebault and La Vallée Tanôt and rejoined 3 Parachute Brigade at La Haie Tondue. The entire brigade was then pulled from the advance and given a well-deserved forty-eight-hour rest.

During this brief interlude, Lieutenant-Colonel Bradbrooke, the 1 Cdn Para Bn's commanding officer relinquished command of the paratroop unit to fill a staff appointment at higher headquarters. He was temporarily replaced by Major G.F. Eadie.

On 25 August 1944, 1 Cdn Para Bn once again assumed the offensive and participated in the attack on Mon Mauger. The following day, the enemy withdrew and the paratroopers liberated the town. This was the Battalion's final operation of the Normandy Campaign.

On 4 September, the Battalion began its departure from France and returned to its "home" in Bulford three

days later. 1 Cdn Para Bn had distinguished itself during the Normandy Campaign — at great cost. During the three-month period between 6 June and 6 September 1944, the Battalion sustained heavy losses. Of the original 443 paratroops dropped, 83 were killed, 187 were wounded and 87 became prisoners of war.

The Battalion's return to England now allowed for an opportunity to rebuild and prepare for the next mission. Not surprisingly, its first priority was to integrate the reinforcements from 1 Cdn Para Training Company into the depleted unit. As the Battalion was being brought up to strength, Lieutenant-Colonel J. A. Nicklin, the new commanding officer, finalized the unit's training plan. Nicklin focussed on correcting the deficiencies and shortcomings noted during the Normandy Campaign, specifically on those skills required for offensive operations. The training schedule included an emphasis on weapons handling, physical fitness, rapid clearance of drop zones, the efficient execution of offensive and defensive battle drills, and street fighting.

During this period the Battalion also received an invaluable windfall. The disbandment of the First Special Service Force on 5 December 1944, at Villeneuve-Louvet, France, provided 1 Cdn Para Bn with additional parachute-trained and battle-hardened reinforcements. And not a moment too soon. On 20 December 1944, Lieutenant-Colonel Nicklin issued a warning order to the Battalion to be ready for active duty.

In mid December 1944, the Germans launched a surprise offensive in the Ardennes of France which became known as the Battle of the Bulge. To counter this German onslaught, all available Allied troops were pressed in battle. As a result, on Christmas Day, elements of the 6th UK Airborne Division, which included 1 Cdn Para Bn, sailed for Ostende, Belgium. The Battalion was then transported to a series of villages around Taintignes, south of Tournai. After a few days the paratroopers were moved to Rochefort, a village on the east bank of the Meuse River. There, they prepared defensive positions and conducted active patrolling until 13 January.

Even though combat had been limited to only minor encounters with the enemy, the 1 Cdn Para Bn earned the distinction of having been the only Canadian combat unit to see action in the Ardennes.

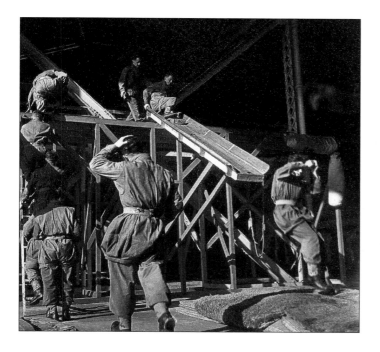

Clockwise from top left: Canadian paratroopers undergoing initial conversion training to British parachuting techniques, October 1943. The slide apparatus was used to practise the side rolling landing technique. (*Sgt E.R. Bonter, NA, PA191121*); British paratroopers practising exit drills from a mock Armstrong-Whitworth "Whitley" aircraft. (*Photographer unknown, NA, PA205029*); Pte L.J. Grenier hones his shooting skills on a rifle range in Bulford on 5 January 1944. The unit's glaring weakness in marksmanship ability prompted Brigadier Hill to bring in a Small Arms Instructor from "Bisley" to raise the unit's performance up to 3 Parachute Brigade standard. (*Sgt E.R. Bonter, NA, PA204957*); British paratroopers spring into action upon landing. At this early stage, in September 1942, weapons were dropped in canisters. (*Photographer unknown, NA, PA205025*)

Pte D.M. Morrison upgrading his small arms skills.

(Photographer unknown, NA, PA198342)

Top: Canadian paratroopers await their turn to jump from the static balloon as part of their conversion training, 5 January 1944. The drop was usually conducted from 800 feet. *(Sgt E.R. Bonter, NA, PA209958)*
Bottom: British paratrooper displaying standard infantry equipment (fall 1943) that was adopted by 1 Cdn Para Bn, in England. Distinctive to the paratroopers were the para helmet, Denison smock, and toggle rope. This paratrooper also carries a 2" mortar.

(1 Cdn Para Bn Assn, Imperial War Museum, BH 24889 XT)

Once the immediate crisis had dissipated and the German advance was checked, the Battalion moved to Holland. By 22 January 1945, 1 Cdn Para Bn had established a series of defensive positions on the west bank of the Meuse River. On the opposite side of the water obstacle, German troops manned a network of well-fortified defensive positions which were part of the vaunted Siegfried Line. In the span of the next two weeks, aggressive patrolling to test the enemy's defensive positions on the east bank of the river ensured daily contacts. The Battalion continued in this fashion until it was relieved in mid February by American forces.

Without having participated in any major operations during its second sojourn in Europe, the Canadian paratroopers returned to Carter Barracks in England on 25 February 1945 to prepare for what would become their final mission.

Following a short leave, the Battalion was brought up to full strength. Not surprisingly, a tough training regimen was once again invoked. Nonetheless, it became apparent that this training interlude would be short. Preparations for an upcoming operation imposed restrictions on the availability of aircraft and specialized airborne equipment for exercises. This in turn created some restraints on the paratroopers. The last time the members of 1 Cdn Para Bn had jumped as a unit was during a training exercise in November 1944. Regardless, the paratroopers were ready to go at a moment's notice.

They did not have long to wait. On 19 March 1945, Battalion personnel were confined to barracks. Morale was high and preparations for what was to be their last airborne assignment were in their final stages.

The Allied High Command was now ready to launch combined Operations Varsity and Plunder. Operation Plunder was the designation for the crossing of the Rhine north of the Ruhr by Allied ground forces. The plan called for a solid bridgehead to be established through which the advance into the heart of the Reich could be launched. Conversely, Operation Varsity was the designation for the airborne assault by the American 17th and British 6th airborne divisions approximately five miles north and northwest of Wesel. The two airborne divisions were responsible for conducting a joint assault to seize the wooded feature which overlooked the Rhine

River at the exact spot where the main assault crossings would be conducted.

The commander of Second Army, Lieutenant-General Miles Dempsey, who was responsible for planning and executing the assault, considered the airborne element essential in the crossing of the Rhine and assigned the two following very simple missions: "1. Seize the commanding ground from which artillery fire controlled the whole area; and 2. Block possible arrival of enemy reinforcements from east of Wesel."

The Allied commanders drew on the collective experiences of all airborne operations conducted to date. The paratroopers would be dropped behind enemy lines in order to seize vital ground, hinder enemy reinforcements, and disrupt the German lines of communications. However, this time the drop would not supercede the main assault but follow it. The explanation for this lay in the reasoning that greater use of firepower could be made to support the ground assault across the Rhine if the artillery and air support were not impeded by paratroopers dropping in the target area. Also deemed important was the necessity of accurately dropping the paratroopers onto their drop zones. Therefore, a daytime jump was preferred.

Within this monumental operation 3 British Parachute Brigade was assigned the task of seizing and clearing a dominating ridge known as the "Schnappenburg feature" and the surrounding Diersfordter Forest. Brigadier Hill stressed the importance of the task on all members of the brigade and stipulated in his orders that "speed and initiative on the part of all ranks is the order of the day, risks will be taken, and the enemy will be attacked and destroyed wherever he is found."

Hill tasked 1 Cdn Para Bn to seize the Hingendahlshof farm on the western edge of the drop zone and to capture the village of Bergerfurth which was located south of the DZ. In short, the Battalion was tasked to hold the central area of the brigade's front, encompassing wooded areas near a road linking Wesel to Emmerich.

In the early evening of 24 March 1945, the Canadian paratroopers emplaned in thirty-five C-47 Dakotas and shortly before 1000 hours the next day, the first of fourteen thousand troops, delivered by a total of seventeen hundred aircraft and thirteen hundred gliders, pierced

L/Cpl Elliott wearing the British "Sorbo" parachute training helmet, has his kit bag release checked prior to a training jump in England, 4 April 1944. *(Sgt E.R. Bonter, NA, PA209959)*

the frontier of the Reich. The brigade, consisting of twenty-two hundred men, dropped with incredible accuracy in a span of only six minutes, in a clearing measuring only 1,000 by 800 yards. 1 Cdn Para Bn jumped at 0955 hours and was met by stiff resistance. The parachute assault experienced devastating fire from the entrenched German positions in the surrounding woods. The clearing was an obvious drop zone and the Germans prepared accordingly.

Despite the resistance, within thirty-five minutes of the drop, eighty-five percent of the brigade had reported in, and the Battalion secured its objectives by 1130 hours, less than two hours from the time they jumped out of their aircraft. The Battalion dug in and repelled numerous probing attacks, but of greater concern was the large number of prisoners which were captured, at one point equalling the strength of the battalion. This quickly became a logistical problem as space for the confinement of prisoners was scarce and guards to secure them were at a premium.

By late evening the lead reconnaissance elements of the 15th Scottish Division moved through the battalion to continue the advance into Germany. In the aftermath of the battle, it was determined that the Battalion's CO, Lieutenant-Colonel Jeff Nicklin had been killed in action. Once again, Major Fraser Eadie took command, this time for good.

For the Battalion, as part of 3 Parachute Brigade, 6th British Airborne Division, the advance through northwest Germany began on 26 March 1945. Field Marshal Montgomery issued a simple directive which set the subsequent pace of events. He stated, "This is the time to take risks and to go 'flat out.' If we reach the Elbe quickly, we win the war." As a result, the offensive onslaught quickly assumed the pattern of advancing during the day, rotating lead by leapfrogging battalions within the brigade and digging in at night. Brigadier Hill pushed the brigade relentlessly. It was evident that he was intent on beating the Russians to Wismar, on the Baltic Sea, in accordance with the direction given to him by Winston Churchill.

The first part of the pursuit involved a rapid push to the Elbe River. So quick was the advance at times that the Canadian paratroopers were transported by trucks or rode on the tanks of the 4th Battalion Grenadiers Guards, 6 Guards Tank Brigade. The paratroopers were regularly called upon to destroy roadblocks and enemy defensive positions, capture bridges, and disarm countless German prisoners who were then sent to the rear to be processed by other troops. The rapid advance was only momentarily halted by imposed forced rest periods, or by the necessity for engineers to erect Bailey bridges. One after another a total of twenty-two towns and villages fell to 1 Cdn Para Bn between 5 to 21 April, 1945. Following a short rest at Kolkhagen, the Battalion commenced the second phase of its final campaign in northwest Europe, namely the advance to the Baltic Sea. The advance was at times so fast that the enemy was simply overrun. However, the rapid tempo also resulted in the brigade outstripping their own supply lines, with the result that the paratroopers quickly resorted to utilizing captured equipment and rations to sustain their progress.

The numbers of fleeing German civilians and surrendering German troops increased dramatically as the Battalion progressed closer to the front lines of the advancing Soviets. The tide of resistance was finally fading and the Germans now indicated a willingness to surrender. The prospect of Soviet occupation and imprisonment was a powerful incentive for capitulation to the Western powers.

By 2 May 1945, 1 Cdn Para Bn had reached Wismar, its final destination. The Battalion secured the town and by nightfall had made contact with the first Russian elements. The Battalion's War Diary recorded the Russian officer's reaction. "It was quite unofficial, since he had no idea we were in Wismar until he came to our barrier. He had come far in advance of his own columns, and was quite put out to find us sitting on what was the Russians' ultimate objective."

The war in Europe was over on 9 May. During the following weeks the Battalion maintained a friendly but firm stance and enforced the Western Allies' policy of holding the Soviet advance at the "gates" of Wismar. By the end of the month the Canadian paratroopers returned to Bulford, England, and impatiently settled into Carter Barracks to await their future.

The British War Office selected the 6th Airborne Division for service in the Far East. Not surprisingly, they requested the retention of 1 Cdn Para Bn. This proposition was studied by both Lieutenant-General J.C. Murchie, the CGS, and Lieutenant-General P.J. Montague, the Chief of Staff, CMHQ. The Canadian generals concluded that the proposition entailed a myriad of administrative difficulties and refused the request. A decision had already been made to disband the unit, and the paratroopers were redeployed to Canada. They disembarked from the *Ile de France* in Halifax on 21 June, the first complete Canadian unit to be repatriated. Lieutenant-Colonel Eadie received the key to the city and a flag of Nova Scotia. Following a parade, the paratroopers were given thirty days' leave and they dispersed to the various parts of the country.

The members of 1 Cdn Para Bn reassembled at Camp Niagara-on-the-Lake, Ontario, in late July. The unit remained in the War Establishment only as An administrative tool. Battalion members were offered the choice of discharge or service in the Far East, but as part of a different unit. The eventual capitulation of Japan in August 1945 rendered the latter offer moot. On 30 September 1945, 1 Canadian Parachute Battalion was officially disbanded.

The nation's first airborne soldiers had earned a proud and remarkable reputation whose legacy would challenge Canada's future paratroopers and imbue them with a special pride. The Battalion never failed to complete an assigned mission, nor did it ever lose or surrender an objective once taken. The Canadian paratroopers were among the first allied soldiers to land in occupied Europe, the only Canadians to participate in the Battle of the Bulge in the Ardennes, and by the end of the war had advanced deeper into Germany than any other Canadian unit. Field Marshal Sir Allan Brooke, Chief of the Imperial General Staff wrote to his Canadian equivalent and stated, "The Battalion played a vital part in the heavy fighting which followed their descent onto French soil in 6 June 1944, during the subsequent critical days and in the pursuit to the Seine. Finally, it played a great part in the lightening pursuit of the German Army right up the shores of the Baltic. It can indeed be proud of its record."

And so, the paratroopers of 1 Canadian Parachute Battalion, 1 Canadian Parachute Training Company/ Battalion and the A-35 Canadian Parachute Training Centre laid, at a great cost and personal sacrifice, the cornerstone of the Canadian Airborne heritage and tradition.

Mass drop for Exercise Cooperation in England, 7 February 1944.

(1 Cdn Para Bn Assn, donated by G. Markewich)

Canadian parachutist exiting a Douglas C-47 Dakota aircraft, 4 April 1944, at RAF Parachute School, Ringway. *(Sgt E.R. Bonter, NA, PA115865)*

"Sweat saves Blood." Training in full gear in England shortly before D-Day. Left to right are Jack Baxter, Phee, Nelson Macdonald, and Carl Baxter.   (*1 Cdn Para Bn Assn*)

First priority of the light infanteer - take care of your feet. Members of 1 Cdn Para Bn take a rest during one of the many forced marches in England. From left to right are Shank, Villeneuve, Haveland.

(*1 Cdn Para Bn Assn, donated by J.A. Shank*)

Members of 1 Cdn Para Bn pose for a picture following a training exercise in England at Carter Barracks. The paratroopers are wearing experimental load-carrying vests for Bren gun magazines.   (*1 Cdn Para Bn Assn*)

"Somewhere in England." Members of 1 Cdn Para Bn in the UK prior to D-Day. Standing, left to right are: Kerman, Phee, Philipps, O. Lynch, Frank Mowat. Kneeling, left to right are: Paul Gervais, Kelly, Hamelin. *(1 Cdn Para Bn Assn, donated by A. Heggie)*

This aerial photo depicts the DZ and actual objectives (circled in grease pencil) of 1 Cdn Para Bn for Exercise Cooperation. The aim of the training, designed specifically in preparation for the Normandy invasion, was to practise landing the maximum number of troops in the smallest possible area in the shortest period of time. *(1 Cdn Para Bn Assn, donated by Bob Firlotte)*

Her Royal Highness, Queen Elizabeth I speaks to Maj D.J. Wilkins, 1 Cdn Para Bn. Brigadier James Hill is in the centre and Princess Elizabeth is in the background, Bulford, May 1944.

(*Sgt E.R. Bonter, NA, PA193086*)

Sniper demonstration for the Royal visit.   *(Photographer unknown, NA, PA179150)*

1st CANADIAN PARACHUTE BATTALION. (C.A.O.)
January 1944. C. COY

Panora Ltd., London, W.C.1.

Pathfinders, the "eyes and ears" of the battalion. Group photo of "C" Company, 1 Cdn Para Bn. They were the first elements of the battalion to land in Europe with the critical task of securing and marking the various drop zones. *(1 Cdn Para Bn Assn, Panora Ltd., London, Negative 29265)*

Canadian paratroopers in their staging area prior to D-Day. Two individuals from the Victory Rifle Platoon stand in the background with their distinctive haircuts. They were actually two of nine paratroopers who had their hair cut to spell out the word "Victory" and the equivalent Morse Code symbols. The individuals, Pte N.V. Wilson and Sgt B.D. Pym, pictured here show the letters "I" and the "V" respectively. *(1 Cdn Para Bn Assn, donated by Bob Firlotte)*

The glider fields of Ranville, France after the second D-Day lift had been completed. A few "Rommelspargeln"anti-glider piquets are still visible. *(1 Cdn Para Bn Assn, Imperial War Museum)*

A brief rest following the battle at Varaville, in Normandy, 6 June 1944.
(1 Cdn Para Bn Assn, donated by John Ross)

The fatigue of battle is plainly evident on the face of L/Cpl John Ross as he waits for the inevitable German counter-attack on D-Day at Varaville.
(1 Cdn Para Bn Assn, donated by John Ross)

The Robehomme Bridge, Normandy. This was the D-Day objective of 5 Platoon, "B" Coy.
(1 Cdn Para Bn Assn, donated by J.M. Kemp)

Airborne medic, W.S. Ducker tends to a wounded German PoW on D-Day. Two weeks later, on 19 June 1944, Ducker himself died of wounds.

(1 Can Para Bn Assn, donated by John Ross)

Fatigue, the soldier's constant companion, is clearly evident in the face of this Canadian paratrooper standing ready to oppose the inevitable German counter-attack. A Mills M-36 defensive grenade is in the foreground.
(*1 Cdn Para Bn Assn, donated by J.J. Miklos*)

Composite / panoramic photograph taken from L/Cpl John Ross' trench in front of the gate house at Varaville. The picture shows Germans surrendering on the left side of the picture, and being disarmed on the right side.
(*1 Cdn Para Bn Assn, donated by John Ross*)

Paratrooper from 1 Cdn Para Bn talks with a member of the Maquis, Normandy, 8 June 1944.
(*D.A. Reynolds, NA, PA129045*)

Canadian paratroopers dig-in along a road in Normandy, France, 8 June 1944.
(*D.A. Reynolds, NA, PA130154*)

Fatigue is clearly evident in the eyes and faces of "Spike and Lee" during the Normandy Campaign in France.

(1 Cdn Para Bn Assn, donated by John Feduck)

Sgt Evans and the remnants of 3 Platoon prepare for a "bath parade" in France on the occasion of being pulled out of the front lines, 4-20 July 1944, for the first time since the invasion.

(1 Cdn Para Bn Assn, donated by John Feduck)

Universal "Bren Gun" carriers mounting .50 calibre machine guns used to support the infantry during the breakout of the Normandy salient.

(1 Cdn Para Bn Assn, donated by John Feduck)

Reinforcements for Normandy at the Bulford Siding, England, 8 August 1944.

(1 Cdn Para Bn Assn, donated by J.J. Miklos)

A patrol from 1 Cdn Para Bn prepares to leave friendly lines near Roy, Belgium, 13 January 1945.

(*Sgt C. H. Lattion, NA, PA191136*)

A formation of C-47 Dakota aircraft ferrying Allied Airborne forces during OP Varsity, the crossing of the Rhine River, 24 March 1945.

(Ken Bell, NA, PA137342)

No turning back. Paratroopers of 1 Cdn Para Bn en route to Germany during OP Varsity, 24 March 1945.

(Photographer unknown, CFPU CNL Neg. PMR78-513)

An Airborne Bren gunner and PIAT anti-tank team remain vigilant on the edge of the woods skirting the DZ, 24 March 1945.

(1 Cdn Para Bn Assn, donated by E. Makela)

A lone paratrooper stands beside a British Airspeed Horsa Troop Glider on the LZ near Wesel, Germany, 24 March 1945.

(1 Cdn Para Bn Assn, donated by D. Fairborne)

Penetrating the Reich. Airborne troops move along the edge of the drop zone following the end of German resistance during OP Varsity.

(Canadian Airborne Forces Museum, (CAFM)

A Sherman "Firefly" and M3 Halftrack, representing the first reconnaissance elements of the 15th Scottish Division, reach 1 Cdn Para Bn, late 24 March 1945.   (*1 Cdn Para Bn Assn, donated by E. Makela*)

The inevitable consequence of war. 1 Cdn Para Bn personnel gather up their dead, 24 March 1945.
(*1 Cdn Para Bn Assn, donated by T. Claphem*)

The main body of the 15th Scottish Division linked-up with the Canadian paratroopers at approximately 0430 hours, 25 March 1945, Bergerfarth Wald, Germany. Pte F.M. Estok greets Lt J.E. Foley.

(*Lt C.H. Richer, NA, PA145734*)

The "morning after." Brewing up prior to commencing the advance into the heart of the Reich. *(1 Cdn Para Bn Assn, donated by E. Makela)*

After the Battle. Cpl C.J. Scott (brushing teeth) and Pte R.D. Amaolo (shaving) use a pause in the war to conduct personal ablutions, Bergerfarth Wald, 25 March 1945. *(Lt C.H. Richer, NA, PA151491)*

After the Battle. Sid Carignan, Bob Surtee, and Morley White (left to right) from 1 Section, 1 Platoon, "A" Company, share a shell scrape on the edge of the DZ during Operation Varsity. *(1 Cdn Para Bn Assn)*

Into the heart of the Reich. Paratroopers advance relentlessly to the Baltic Sea. *(1 Cdn Para Bn Assn)*

Top and opposite page: Race to the sea. British Prime Minister Churchill gave his senior commanders firm direction to beat the Russians to the Baltic. To accomplish this, tanks were quickly converted to taxis. *(Lt C.H. Richer, NA, PA191134)*

Paratroopers converted to "Panzer Grenadiers"

(*Lt C.H. Richer, NA, PA142610*)

Paratroopers enjoy a break from marching in their race to the sea.

(1 Cdn Para Bn Assn, donated by Jan de Vries)

The relentless pursuit. Exhausted paratroopers take a much-needed break. Brigadier Hill noted that all the physical training conducted in England "gave us an invaluable asset - Endurance." *(1 Cdn Para Bn Assn, donated by Jan de Vries)*

Pte R.A. Boicey cleans his pistol during a pause in the advance in Lembeck, Germany, 29 March 1945. *(Lt C.H. Richer, NA, PA137325)*

The consequences of total war, Coesfeld after the advance, 30 March 1945.

(*Lt C.H. Richer, NA, PA205202*)

Cdn Para Bn Mortar Platoon personnel preparing for action in Germany, April 1945.

(1 Cdn Para Bn Assn, donated by G. Markewich)

Canadian Forward Observation officers attached to the 6th Airborne Division in Greven, Germany, 5 April 1945. *(Lt C.H. Richer, NA, PA162854)*

Masters of improvisation. Members of 1 Cdn Para Bn use a gas railway buggy for transportation in Greven, Germany, 5 April 1945. *(Lt C.H. Richer, NA, PA162853)*

Ptes M.C. Ballance and R.S. Phillips fry eggs on the exhaust of a Churchill tank, Wiedensahl, Germany, 1 April 1945. *(Lt C.H. Richer, NA, PA145971)*

P.L. Johnson and Sgt D.R. Fairborn with a PIAT Gun in Lembeck, Germany, 29 March 1945.

(Lt C.H. Richer, NA, PA114595)

Members of 1 Cdn Para Bn continue the advance from Greven, Germany, on bicycles, 5 April 1945. *(Lt C.H. Richer, NA, PA205204)*

The relentless advance. 1 Cdn Para Bn in the village of Luthe, Germany, 8 April 1945. *(Lt C.H. Richer, NA, PA205205)*

LCol Fraser Eadie inspects the Battalion, 24 April 1945, in Kolkhagen, Germany, in accordance with Brigadier Hill's insistence on maintaining order and discipline regardless of the surroundings. With the war practically won, a return to a more disciplined deportment took on a higher priority.

(Lt C.H. Richer, NA, PA204981)

A vanquished army.

(1 Cdn Para Bn Assn, donated by D. Morrison)

West meets East. Link-up with the Soviets at Wismar on the Baltic Sea, 4 May 1945.
(Lt C.H. Richer, NA, PA150930)

Clockwise from top left; Members of 1 Cdn Para Bn (Scott, Sutherland, Peerless) with three Soviet airmen at Wismar, Germany, May 1945. *(1 Cdn Para Bn Assn, donated by J. Peerless)*; Cpl F.G. Topham and Pte A. Pakulak pose in Kolkhagen, Germany, April 1945. *(1 Cdn Para Bn Assn, donated by Irvine Van Horne)*; Wishful thinking. *(1 Cdn Para Bn Assn, donated by E. Makela)*; Ptes G.L. Wetherup and K.D. Wolfe from 1 Cdn Para Bn stand guard over the Reichbank at Wismar, 7 May 1945. *(Lt C.H. Richer, NA, PA204961)*

CQMS H. I. Smith from 1 Cdn Para Bn, sporting an American M1 A1 .30 calibre carbine with metal folding stock, and sheepskin coat, Germany, April 1945.

(1 Cdn Para Bn Assn, donated by D. Morrison)

"End of the Road - Victory in Europe." Members of 1 Cdn Para Bn prepare to return to England to await repatriation to Canada.

(1 Cdn Para Bn Assn, donated by D. Morrison and G. Markewich)

A tumultuous welcome was given to the returning Airborne warriors by the City of Toronto. *(1 Cdn Para Bn Assn, donated by Wilf DeLory)*

Top and middle: "End of the Road - Victory in Europe." Members of 1 Cdn Para Bn prepare to return to England to await repatriation to Canada. *(1 Cdn Para Bn Assn, donated by D. Morrison and G. Markewich)*; bottom: The *Isle de France* returning the paratroopers to Canada. The ship landed in Halifax. *(1 Cdn Para Bn Assn, donated by Wilf DeLory)*

PART III

POSTWAR DEVELOPMENTS

AN ARMY IN TRANSITION, 1946-1967

pring 1945 not only brought the end of the Second World War, but seemingly also terminated Canada's foray with airborne forces. The senior Army leadership's decision to disband 1 Canadian Parachute Battalion was made with no intention to replace it or the capability it represented. The long costly global struggle had taken its toll and a debt-ridden and war-weary government was intent on a postwar army which was anything but extravagant.

Notwithstanding the military's achievements during the war, the government had but two requirements for its peacetime army. First, it was to consist of a representative group of all arms of the service. Second, its primary purpose was to provide a small but highly trained and skilled professional force which, in time of conflict, could expand and train the citizen soldiers who would fight that war. Within this framework, paratroopers had limited relevance. Predictably, little concern was shown for the potential loss of Canada's hard-earned airborne experience.

In this austere climate of "minimum peacetime obligations," the fate of Canada's airborne soldiers was dubious at best. This should not have

Top and bottom: The visit of the CGS, General H.D.G. Crerar to No. 1 ARDC, in Shilo, 15 January 1946.
(Photographer unknown, NAC,s PA205316, PA205317)

been a surprise to anyone. The training of new para-troopers at the A-35 Canadian Parachute Training Centre (CPTC) in Shilo had ceased as early as May 1945. Despite the school's tenuous future, the commanding officer had had the foresight to recruit the ex-members of 1 Cdn Para Bn and the First Special Service Force. He realized that their wartime airborne experience and their close ties to their American and British colleagues would prove invaluable for future training. In spite of these efforts, the survival of the CPTC still hung in the air, pending the final decision on the structure of the postwar army.

Nevertheless, the parachute school, largely on its own initiative, worked to keep abreast of airborne developments in other countries. Specifically, the CPTC worked hard at perpetuating the links with American and British airborne units that had been forged in the furnace of the Second World War. Fortuitously, the importance of remaining current in regard to the latest tactical developments in modern warfare, specifically air-transportability, as well as of conserving ties with Canada's closest allies, provided the breath of life that the airborne advocates desperately needed. An NDHQ study tabled late in 1945 revealed that both the Americans and the British were emphasizing the importance of airborne/air-transported training in regard to their postwar infantry formations. The report further noted that both of these allies would welcome an airborne establishment in Canada that would be capable of "filling in the gaps in their knowledge."

These "gaps" included the problem of standardization of equipment between Britain and the United States, and the need for experimental research into cold-weather conditions. Canada was seen as the ideal intermediary for both. It was not lost on the Canadian study team that co-operation with its allies would allow Canada to benefit from an exchange of information on the latest defence developments and doctrine. A test facility was not an airborne unit, but it would allow the Canadian military to stay in the game. Therefore, with an eye for efficiency of manpower and resources, the senior military leadership decided to combine the No.1 Airborne Research and Development Centre with the Parachute Training School. As a result, on 15 April 1947,

NDHQ authorized the formation of the Joint Air School (JAS) in Rivers, Manitoba.

The Joint Air School received a very inclusive mandate. It was responsible for: research in airportability of Army personnel and equipment; user trials of equipment, especially under cold weather conditions; limited development and assessment of airborne equipment; training of paratroop volunteers; training in airportability of personnel and equipment; advanced training of glider pilots in exercises with troops; and training in some of the uses of light aircraft.

The Joint Air School became the "foot in the door." Quite simply, its function was to ensure the retention of the necessary skills for airborne operations for both the Army and the RCAF. More importantly, the JAS provided the seed from which an airborne organization could grow.

Predictably, it was not long before the impetus for expansion of the negligible Canadian parachute capability began to emerge. The growth manifested itself in the form of a proposed Canadian Special Air Service (SAS) Company. Its origin and existence remain enigmatic. The establishment of the SAS Company was proposed in 1947 by the Joint Air School with the support of the Canadian Army. In fact, the organization was to be an integral sub-unit of the Army component of the JAS. Its purpose was defined as filling a need to perform Army, inter-service, and public duties such as army/air tactical research and development; demonstrations to assist with army/air training; airborne firefighting; search and rescue; and aid to the civil power. The importance of these missions in support of the national and public interest was highlighted during the planning phase of the SAS Company. Its potential was demonstrated in the fall of 1947, when a four- man team headed by Captain Lionel Guy D'Artois was called upon to participate in Operation Canon, the designation for the rescue mission of Canon John H. Turner, an Anglican missionary who worked out of an isolated outpost located in Moffet Inlet, Baffin Island.

Turner had sustained a serious injury due to a firearm accident and was in need of immediate medical attention. D'Artois's team parachuted onto a small frozen lake in the vicinity of the Inlet on 3 October 1947. After a two-and-a-half-hour walk over the tundra,

D'Artois solicited the aid of a trapper and two Inuit and went by boat to Bartlett Inlet to retrieve the rest of his team still waiting on the drop zone. As suspected, Canon Turner's condition was critical. However, severe weather conditions, heavy ice floes, and a radio set damaged as a result of the initial drop hampered the rescue effort.

A sea evacuation was impossible, and as a result D'Artois was forced to scour the formidable environs by dog sled in search of an expedient airstrip. A suitable landing site was eventually located, but once again weather conditions deteriorated.

For two days, D'Artois was forced to camp on the landing site in severe conditions. Finally, on 21 November, Turner and his family, as well as the rescue team, were evacuated to Winnipeg aboard a C-47 Dakota piloted by Captain Robert C. Race. Despite the heroic efforts and the epic fifty-one-day adventure, Canon Turner succumbed to his wounds and passed away on 7 December 1947. Nonetheless, Captain D'Artois had demonstrated the potential of the parachute capability and a few good men.

But this was a moot point; the proposal had already been forwarded to Ottawa through the Army chain of command. Surreptitiously, as the proposal worked its way through the labyrinth of NDHQ, two additional roles were added to the SAS Company, apparently by the NDHQ Director of Weapons and Development. One was an innocuous "public service in the event of a national catastrophe." The other was the "provision of a nucleus for expansion into parachute battalions."

The dramatic change in focus became even more evident once authorization to establish the Canadian SAS Company was formalized. Not only did its function as a base for expansion take precedence, but also a hitherto unmentioned war-fighting role emerged. The new terms of reference for the SAS Company now detailed a revised priority of employment. Primary importance was given to the requirement to provide a tactical parachute company for airborne training which would form the nucleus for expansion of three active force infantry units into parachute battalions. Second, the SAS Company was mandated to provide a formed body of troops to participate in tactical exercises and demonstrations for courses at the Joint Air School and service units throughout the country. Third, a new war-fighting role, specifically "to preserve and advance the techniques of SAS [commando] operations developed during WW II 1939-1945," was added. Relegated to peripheral status were the requirements to provide, when necessary, parachutists to back up the RCAF organizations as detailed in the Interim Plan for Air Search and Rescue and the demand to aid civil authorities in fighting forest fires and assisting in national catastrophes as directed by Defence Headquarters. Although this change in focus did raise concern with some staff officers in Ottawa, a certain degree of naïveté on their part was present.

The name chosen for the sub-unit was clear evidence of the true intent. Equally so was the 1948 Annual Historical Report for the Joint Air School Army Component. The document clearly stated, "during World War II the [British] SAS was formed to attack military targets, including airfields, behind the enemy lines. They operated in small parties in uniform, and whether they arrived at their destination by sea, air or land was immaterial. To operate behind enemy lines it was necessary to have men finely trained and utterly reliable." Although a certain amount of conjecture is required, it appears that the original civic-minded tasks given for the SAS Company were designed more to ensure high-level military and political approval than they were to represent the true motive of the intended role of the sub-unit.

It must be remembered that the Army component of the JAS at this time was staffed almost exclusively by airborne veterans who felt strongly that a viable parachute capability was required in the Army. In the short term their desires were filled.

The SAS Company was officially authorized on 9 January 1948. Its strength was 125 personnel, and it consisted of a platoon from each of the active force infantry regiments, namely the Royal Canadian Regiment (RCR), the Royal 22e Regiment (R22eR), and Princess Patricia's Canadian Light Infantry (PPCLI). Operationally, the sub-unit provided a unique national quick-reaction capability. The Joint Air School Commander, who was responsible for the employment

Parachute training hanger with "mock-ups" visible
within. *(B.A.J. Franklin)*

"Leo's Leap." Ground training, practising landing rolls, prior to "J" Phase. *(B.A.J. Franklin)*

Four paratroopers at Stevenson Field, Ipperwash, Ontario during a rehearsal for an RCAF airshow, July
1946. *(Photographer unknown, NA, PA204969)*

of the SAS Company, required the sub-unit to be capable of deploying anywhere in Canada within ten to fifteen hours.

Although debate over the nature and role of the SAS continued within Defence Headquarters in Ottawa, for the men who were recruited there was no question about their commando persona. The acting Company Commander, Captain D'Artois, a wartime veteran of the First Special Service Force, and the Special Operations Executive (SOE) reinforced this notion. Much to the despair of his superior officers at Rivers, D'Artois pursued a relentless emphasis on the specialized warfighting role instead of on the more benign public service focus. Nevertheless, in spite of D'Artois's efforts, at least one platoon of the company was normally tasked on "demonstration" duties across the country because of the Joint Air School Commander's emphasis on providing demonstrations on airborne/air-transportability operations for the military, as well as the public.

The SAS Company's future, however, was tenuous. Debate over its ultimate role was overshadowed by more pressing circumstances.

By the summer of 1948, the Army Command directed that the sub-unit be prepared to form the nucleus for the establishment of parachute battalions. This turn of events was not due to a belated belief in airborne forces but rather to a consequence of political reality. The resurrection of a viable national airborne capability was inextricably tied to the American concern for Canada's northern regions and the avenue of approach that they perceived it to represent. The threat of a Soviet invasion over the polar icecap forced the Canadian government to find a cost-efficient, yet credible, response which would reassure the United States that its ally was capable of securing the exposed "northern flank" from enemy lodgements. Once again, the issue of defending and monitoring the North became a top-priority defence issue for the American military commanders and politicians alike. Seared in their psyche were the haunting spectres of the Japanese attack on Pearl Harbor and the enemy occupation of several islands in the Aleutians during the Second World War.

The deteriorating relations with the Soviets, particularly in Central Europe, and the failure of the communists to demobilize their enormous wartime military machine spurred the American anxiety. The Canadian government, however, did not share the American threat assessment, particularly on the issue of the perceived vulnerability of the Arctic to Soviet invasion. Confidential Canadian military and political intelligence analysis continually dismissed the likelihood of Soviet intention or capability in regard to hostile action against Canadian territory.

Nevertheless, fresh in the minds of Canadian politicians, particularly that of Prime Minister Mackenzie King, was the experience of the joint American-Canadian northern defence ventures of the recent global struggle. Scorched in the Canadian consciousness was the fact that the "joint ventures" quickly turned into American-dominated, if not entirely controlled, operations. Therefore, Prime Minister King's Liberal government wanted to ensure that any future defence effort in the North would be strictly Canadian. The quandary, however, was how to placate their ally's concerns, namely convince the Americans that the northern flank was adequately safeguarded by Canada, yet keep defence spending at the lowest possible level.

Furthermore, in accordance with the 1946 Canadian/US Basic Security Plan (BSP), the Canadian government was obligated, by 1 May 1949, to have a battalion combat team prepared to respond immediately to any actual enemy lodgement, with a second battalion available within two months, and an entire brigade group within four months. As a result, the government announced in 1946 that airborne training for the active-force brigade group was planned with the aim of creating a peacetime Army structure based on an airborne/air-transportable formation.

This seemed to fulfill the government's requirement. It provided a very mobile force which could respond rapidly to any threat to its territory in accordance with the obligations of the 1946 BSP. Moreover, since the Canadian government dismissed the possibility of an actual Soviet attack on the North, it could maintain this force as a "paper tiger" and thus keep defence costs down.

The reality of this cynical interpretation is based on the fact that the government refused to authorize the

Sgts H.C. Cook and W.W. Judd, two signalmen who parachuted into Moffet Inlet on 4 October 1947 to set up wireless communications for the evacuation of Canon J. Turner enjoy a cup of coffee on their arrival in Winnipeg, Manitoba.

(Capt Dubervill, NAC, PA189547)

Flying Officer Bob Race (pilot of the evacuation aircraft), Capt Guy D'Artois, and Capt Ross Willoughby (medical officer) pose for a picture in Winnipeg, after their dramatic rescue mission. *(Capt Dubervill, NAC, PA189545)*

military's proposals for actually implementing this force.

Finally, in the spring of 1948 General Charles Foulkes, the Chief of the General Staff, became concerned with the lack of progress which had been made toward the BSP obligation. It had been two years since the government had made its announcement and yet with the exception of the SAS Company, nothing had been done to achieve the airborne/air-transportable active-force brigade. The CGS, fully aware of the government's antipathy towards defence spending, now recommended a slower approach. Rather than convert the Army all at once, the program would be implemented in phases.

This seemed to break the log jam. The government now gave its approval and action was immediately taken. On 9 August 1948, Major-General C.C. Mann, the Vice Chief of the General Staff, visited the PPCLI Battalion in Calgary and asked them to convert to airborne status. The response was enthusiastic and unanimous. As a result, the PPCLI became the first active-force infantry regiment to undergo parachute and air-transportability training. In accordance with the phased plan, upon completion of the conversion of the PPCLI, the RCR and then the R22eR would begin their transformation to airborne status in 1950 and 1951 respectively. With the termination of the R22eR's conversion, the infantry component of the Canadian Army's airborne/air-transportable brigade group would be complete. This force, in conjunction with similarly trained support arms, became known as the Mobile Striking Force (MSF). Albeit later than required by the Basic Security Plan, the scheme enunciated in 1946 was finally being implemented.

The impact of the formation of the MSF on the SAS Company was profound. Following Mann's announcement, the SAS Company personnel became parachute-instructor (PI) qualified. Initially, the MSF conversion plan called for the members of each platoon to serve as PIs for their respective parent regiments. The reality became less palatable for the individuals in the SAS Company. The SAS PPCLI platoon was the first to undergo the new task. Predictably, the PPCLI demanded that their SAS personnel remain with the parent unit and return to Calgary upon completion of the conversion training.

Although the "Patricia" platoon was replaced in the SAS Company by another platoon recruited from the support trades within the Army Field Force, the precedent was set. As each battalion completed their airborne training, they retained their PIs. But, this mattered little because by the time the R22eR had begun their conversion training, the SAS Company had already disintegrated. Nonetheless, its role had been key. The SAS Company became Canada's interim measure. It provided the military with a provisional response and a cadre for expansion. However, once the commencement of conversion training for the infantry battalions of the MSF began in October 1948, the end of the SAS Company was clearly imminent. Increasingly, its personnel were drafted as instructional staff for the Joint Air School/Canadian Joint Air Training Centre (CJATC) training program, which was focussed on converting the three active-force infantry battalions into airborne/air-transportable units. By the time the scheme was terminated, the SAS Company had ceased to exist. Its highly trained personnel were returned to their parent regiments for service in the newly converted airborne battalions.

Although the SAS Company existed for less than two years, its place in the nation's airborne history cannot be underestimated. It became the "airborne bridge" which spanned the gap between 1 Canadian Parachute Battalion and the airborne battalions of the Mobile Striking Force. As such, it played a critical role in ensuring that the requisite parachute skills stayed alive, as well as perpetuating the indomitable airborne spirit.

The expansion of Canada's airborne capability, however, did not represent a wholesale change in philosophy by the military or political leadership in regard to airborne forces. The MSF's existence reflected the lethargy and hesitancy which went into its implementation. It represented a political expedient rather than a hard operational requirement. From its inception, the MSF encountered a series of never-ending obstacles. As already noted, the politicians were not convinced that the Soviets would, or even could, launch large-scale ground operations in the Arctic. Senior military officers on the whole agreed with this assessment. Furthermore, with an already limited budget there were no immediate funds available to provide the new parachute force with the required air transport and specialized airborne equipment. Therefore, it is no surprise that support for an operational concept which was not considered credible by the military and political leadership remained minimal.

The MSF's questionable status was evident from the very beginning. A test exercise, Exercise Eagle, was conducted in August 1949 to assess the operational efficiency of the newly converted PPCLI Battalion. The scenario depicted an airborne deployment of a small lightly armed "Russian" force landing and capturing the Fort St. John Airfield and the Peace River Bridge in British Columbia. The PPCLI, as part of a larger joint Canadian-US task force, was directed to destroy the enemy lodgement. The Patricias were specifically given the mission of conducting a parachute assault to seize the airstrip at Fort St. John Airfield and support the airlanding of the remainder of the battalion. Success was not realized and the exercise resulted in a serious blow to the reputation of the fledgling Mobile Striking Force. The parachute drop onto the intended drop zone was poorly executed. Paratroopers were widely dispersed, most missing the actual target. In addition, the "enemy's" ability to gain and maintain air superiority further reduced the effectiveness of the MSF paratroopers. Post-exercise reports also revealed that the paratroopers were not properly equipped and had to borrow parachutes and other pieces of equipment from the Canadian Joint Air Training Centre (formerly Joint Air School).

The government, in particular the Minister of National Defence, Brooke Claxton, was severely embarrassed by the poor showing. The political opposition in Parliament, as well as the press, denounced Canada's military ill-preparedness and the government's negligence in leaving the North undefended.

As a direct result of the criticism, Claxton launched an immediate campaign to redeem his reputation, as well as that of the government. The first step of the program was the appointment of Brigadier George Kitching as the Commander Designate of the Mobile Striking Force. General Foulkes, the CGS, gave Kitching and his small staff the task of preparing comprehensive operational plans for the defence of the North. More importantly, Claxton directed the new MSF Commander Designate to ensure that another test exercise was conducted. Implicit

in the direction was the requirement to ensure it was successful!

The attempt at redemption took the form of Exercise Sweetbriar in February 1950. This combined American-Canadian exercise was once again conducted along the Alaska Highway, with a scenario analogous to that of Exercise Eagle. An enemy force had ostensibly captured an airfield in Northway, Alaska and was proceeding to advance along the Alaska Highway towards Whitehorse, Yukon. The joint Canadian-US force was given the mission to counter and destroy the enemy units. The allied endeavour was declared a complete success. Brooke Claxton quickly asserted the government's ability to defend Canadian territory and emphatically pronounced that the latest demonstration vindicated the MSF's viability in regard to the defence of the North.

But Exercise Sweetbriar represented the zenith of the Mobile Striking Force. Ironically, the MSF's apex came before it was even fully constituted. The RCR and R22eR battalions had not yet fully completed their conversion training. Moreover, Exercise Sweetbriar was the last MSF or formation-level manoeuvre. Henceforth, all "MSF/Defence of Canada" exercises were limited occasionally to unit, but more normally to sub-unit level. This was due to the lack of credibility of the MSF's role. The political leadership, as well as many senior military commanders dismissed the threat to the North, and as a result the requirement for viable and costly airborne forces. To exacerbate the MSF's problems, the formation of the North Atlantic Treaty Organization (NATO) in 1949 and the conflict in Korea in 1950 gave the Canadian military new commitments on which to focus.

This turn of events destroyed any hope of the MSF becoming an operationally effective entity. The politicians viewed the Mobile Striking Force as an insurance policy to placate both Canada's anxious American ally and protect its northern territory. However, because of their contempt of the actual threat and their focus on social programs, they demanded the cheapest possible premium. Similarly, military commanders originally looked upon the Mobile Striking Force as a means to justify and protect peacetime organizations and equipment requests. But, the new NATO role, which included large modern, mechanized forces to be stationed in Europe, as well as the

SAS paratroopers practising exit drills, January 1948.   (*Lt Dare, NAC, PA166961*)

"Flight" training, January 1948.   (*Lt Dare, NAC, PA205013*)

requirement to deploy a brigade-sized field force in Korea, now gave the Army a whole new sense of purpose.

In this new context, the paratroopers of the MSF represented nothing more than a potential drain of limited resources which were required for the more important NATO and UN roles. Therefore, before the MSF was even fully implemented, it became marginalized and was shunted to the periphery of the Canadian Army. The airborne battalions each fielded a parachute company and the remaining personnel within the unit were designated as air-transportable. Although only enough paratroopers to man a sub-unit were required, the Army's priority on the NATO and UN commitments resulted in a chronic shortage of airborne-qualified instructors, equipment and transport aircraft. Furthermore, the MSF-designated units were continually tasked to train recruits for the Korean conflict, as well as to conduct combined arms training in consonance with the new NATO orientation. As a result, MSF training exercises, which were already relegated to unit/sub-unit level, were minimized even more.

Remarkably, the MSF's fortunes declined even further. A changing perception of the threat to North America added yet another nail to the coffin of the Mobile Striking Force. As already indicated, the political leadership viewed the likelihood of a Soviet land invasion via the "exposed northern flank" with contempt, and military commanders dismissed it as impractical. But, by the early fifties, the Soviets had demonstrated that they had the technological expertise to produce atomic weapons and long-range bombers. As a result, the Soviet peril to the North American land mass was now defined almost exclusively as an air threat, a belief shared by both Americans and Canadians and universally accepted by the military leadership, politicians, and the public. This change in perception had a direct and dramatic effect on the paratroopers of the MSF. The Americans no longer placed the same emphasis or interest on the Canadian North. This allowed the Canadian government to further reduce its efforts and resources in the Arctic and correspondingly on the Mobile Striking Force. The only saving grace for the paratroopers was the nebulous concept of "enemy lodgements," which theoretically required a continued parachute capability.

Although intelligence reports and strategic military appreciations emphasized the threat of bombing of North American cities with atomic weapons, they also acknowledged the possibility of Soviet special forces, on the scale of thirty to a hundred personnel, infiltrating Canada by parachute, submarine, or fishing trawler to conduct a campaign of sabotage and terror. Some military analysts also believed that the Soviets would attempt to develop northern airstrips, either on frozen lakes or on existing airfields, as refuelling points for their bombers.

These scenarios provided the MSF with a tenuous existence. Once again the government and military realized it must maintain some form of capability to meet its obligations under the joint Canadian/US Basic Security Plan, and the hollow shell of the Mobile Striking Force provided a political expedient. Its presence represented a capability to defend the North, yet by limiting the resources dedicated to the MSF mandate, it was also cost-effective.

Nevertheless, even this ethereal state of affairs was soon shattered. On 26 August 1957, the Soviets announced that they had successfully launched their first inter-continental ballistic missile (ICBM). This new dimension to the air threat further entrenched the perception that the MSF was irrelevant and had no credible role. Both the military and scientific communities agreed that it was impossible to completely defend against the manned bomber, much less against ICBMs. Therefore, the government's defence policy in regard to the North evolved from one of defence to one of simple surveillance.

The impact was quickly felt by Canada's airborne forces. In January 1958, the Mobile Striking Force was restructured and renamed the Defence of Canada Force (DCF). The reorganization entailed abandoning the airborne battalion structure and instead establishing parachute companies (commonly referred to as "jump companies") within each of the RCR, R22eR and PPCLI infantry regiments. This much-reduced decentralized parachute capability was now responsible for meeting the defence-of-Canada mandate, specifically the response to "enemy lodgements." The dramatic cutback, the lack of a credible role, and a widespread belief within the Army that paratroopers were not relevant in

Endurance training, January 1948.

(Lt Dare, NA, PA205014)

the Canadian context ensured the continuing erosion of the airborne capability.

DCF activities and training continued to suffer from conscious neglect. The Canadian military was completely focussed on NATO and to a lesser degree on United Nations operations. Airborne forces were simply a drain on a limited resource pool. By the mid to late sixties the Defence of Canada Force, as represented by the three decentralized parachute companies, was merely a shell. It did not represent an operational capability, but rather a structure that was simply attempting to keep the art and skill of military parachuting alive.

SAS Coy paratroopers undergoing wind machine training.

(B.A.J. Franklin)

Waco CG-4A gliders over the Cdn SAS Coy quarters, Rivers, 1948. *(B.A.J. Franklin)*

The infamous "wind machine" used to simulate the difficulties of collapsing a parachute upon landing during windy conditions. *(B.A.J. Franklin)*

SAS Coy members, Ptes L.W. Randall and C.E. Buck, dressed for battle with the wind machine. *(B.A.J. Franklin)*

The R22eR Platoon of the SAS Company prepares for troop-carrying trials on a Canadair Lodemaster in the Spring of 1949. This aircraft never went into production. The C-47 Dakota, in use at the time, was superceded by the C-82 Fairchild Packet and later by the C-119 Fairchild Flying Boxcar. *(George Ferris)*

SAS Coy paratroopers, sporting boot knives, emplaning for a practise jump. *(B.A.J. Franklin)*

Members of the R22eR SAS Platoon en route for a drop at Ancienne Lorette, Quebec. *(B.A.J. Franklin)*

Clockwise from top: SAS Coy personnel observe the connecting of the tow cable to the nose of the Waco CG-4A glider. *(B.A.J. Franklin)*; SAS Coy para-drop. *(B.A.J. Franklin)*; Aid to the Civil Power. SAS Coy members assist in building dikes during the British Columbia floods, June 1949, in the Lulu Island area. *(B.A.J. Franklin)*; SAS Coy paratroopers conducting unarmed combat training. *(B.A.J. Franklin)*; A most irrevocable step. *(B.A.J. Franklin)*

Airportabilitiy training at the Joint Air School, Rivers, 8 November 1948.   *(Lt Plastow, NAC, PA205103)*

Airportability course at the JAS, Rivers, January 1948.   *(Lt Dare, NAC, PA205015)*

On 9 August 1948, Other Ranks of the PPCLI respond to the VCGS' request by saluting and saying "I volunteer to be a jumper, Sir." *(Maj Stirton, NAC, PA204973)*

Parachute candidates, executing the "exit" which incorporated a vigorous kick with the right leg, Rivers. *(PPCLI Archives)*

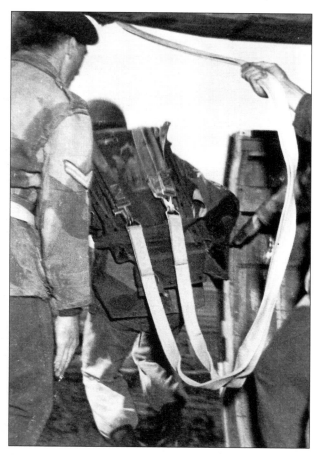

Cpl McGee "tapping" personnel from the Mock Tower to indicate their turn to exit. *(B.A.J. Franklin)*

PPCLI paratroopers conducting an airborne assault during Ex Eagle to capture the airport at Fort St. John, BC, on the Alaska Highway. *(WO 1 Jolly, NA, PA204974)*

PPCLI paratroopers, of the MSF, en route to their objective during Ex Eagle, 6-7 August 1949. *(Photographer unknown, NA, PA179779)*

Glider-borne infantry from the PPCLI land on the rolling banks of the Peace River in readiness for the attack on the Peace River Bridge, on the Alaska Highway, North-West Highway System (NWHS) during Ex Eagle.

(SSgt W.C. Fenwick, NA, PA179781)

A glider-borne PPCLI infantryman adopts a firing position with his Bren gun immediately upon exiting the aircraft. The glider landed near the Peace River Bridge during Ex Eagle.

(Photographer unknown, NA, PA204976)

PPCLI paratroopers secure the approach to the Peace River Bridge prior to its capture, during Ex Eagle.

(SSgt W.C. Fenwick, NA, PA179778)

Paratroopers from the PPCLI clear the objective during the attack on the airfield at Fort St. John, during Ex Eagle.

(Photographer unknown, NA, PA204975)

PPCLI paratroopers, in winter dress, with rifle valises, undergo final JM check prior to boarding their aircraft.
(PPCLI Archives)

PPCLI paratroopers, in non-tactical winter dress, en route to their drop zone, Rivers, Manitoba.
(PPCLI Archives)

Clockwise from top-left: MSF Paratroopers in winter camouflage, participating in Ex Fly Rite, January 1950. (*CAFM*); Paratrooper in white camouflage with released rifle valise preparing to land during Ex Sweetbriar, February 1950. The town of Northway, Alaska, can be seen in the upper left corner. (*PPCLI Archives*); The rationale behind the MSF and DCF defence of the North. 9 Platoon of "C" Coy, (RCR) conducting training in the Arctic. (*Fenn, NA, PA204970*); PPCLI Pathfinders prepare the DZ for the main drop at Northway during Ex Sweetbriar, 23 February 1950. (*Plastow, NA, PA204977*)

Coy of the RCR airborne battalion marches through a section of Algonquin Park during day seven of an exercise, July 1950.
(Capt Cooper, NA, PA204963)

The JAS Rivers jump team with complete equipment load, 6 March 1950.
(PR Prairie Command, NA, PA205101)

Top to bottom: Conversion training to the new C-119 aircraft was conducted 1951-1952. *(B.A.J. Franklin)*

Opposite page: left, top: Airborne Signal Support Unit (ASSU) paratrooper fully loaded with communication equipment. *(Directorate of History and Heritage)*; bottom: Paratroopers exit a C-119 Boxcar for a winter exercise. *(D.L. Harris)*; far right: The Patricias jump into Camp Wainwright during Ex Bulldog IV.
(Sgt Lee, CFPU CNL, Neg. PL 76877)

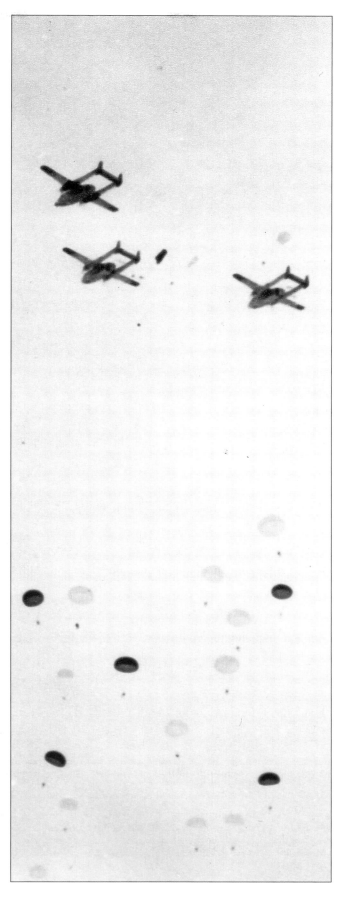

(Photographer unknown, CFPU CNL, Neg. RE78-2949)

(Photographer unknown, NA PA204964)

Three views: MSF paratroopers of the 1st Bn RCR, drop on Malton Airport, near Toronto, Ontario, as part of the Annual Airshow on 15 September 1951. Their objective was to seize the airfield and destroy the radar installation. *(Photographer unknown, NA PA204966)*

The highly renowned High Tower in Rivers, Manitoba, May 1956. This apparatus was used to practise landings.

(Du Cloux, CFPU CNL, Neg. ZK-1637)

"Patricia" jumpers en route to their DZ in Camp Wainwright, during Ex Bulldog IV.

(Cpl Dreidger, CFPU CNL, Neg. PL 76874)

The dreaded "Mock Tower" at CJATC, Rivers, November 1955. This structure provided realism for the training of individuals in aircraft exits.

(Du Cloux, CFPU CNL, Neg. ZK-1821)

A staged photograph depicting a JM's exit inspection prior to dispatching paratroopers, May 1956.

(Du Cloux, CFPU CNL, Neg. ZK-1820)

Paratroopers from the PPCLI board a C-119 Flying Boxcar of 435 Transport Squadron at RCAF Station Namao, Alberta, 3 April 1959.
(Cpl G.L. Abbott, CFPU CNL, Neg. PL 77474)

Twenty-seven paratroopers of the 1st Light Battery (Paratroop) RCA, from Camp Shilo, Manitoba, conduct a water jump into Lake Ontario during the Canadian National Exhibition, 1 September 1952. Before landing in the water the paratroopers pulled a cartridge which inflated their lifebelts.
(WO 1 Jolley, NA, PA204967)

A Captain, from the Queen's Own Rifles of Canada, conducts a JM's inspection of four instructors prior to a training jump, May 1956.
(Du Cloux, CFPU CNL, Neg. ZK-1636)

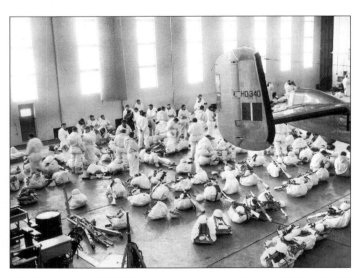

Chalk Assembly. PPCLI paratroopers prepare for Ex Bulldog IV, 15 February 1958, at the Namao Airbase in Edmonton.
(Cpl Gibson, CFPU CNL, Neg. PL 76876)

Two RCR paratroopers conduct a "Landing Swing" practise at Wolseley Barracks, London, Ontario, 1956.

(Royal Canadian Regiment (RCR) Museum)

Paratroopers from the 2nd Battalion PPCLI jump from an RCAF C-119 Flying Boxcar during Ex Snow Chinthe near Cold Lake, Alberta, on 22 February 1960. The exercise was designed to test the effectiveness of Western Army Command and Air Transport Command in winter conditions. *(Cpl G.L. Abbott, CFPU CNL, Neg. PL 77305)*

DCF paratroopers conduct a "Ramp Jump," as part of a tactical exercise on 16 May 1967. *(CAFM)*

PART IV

THE GREAT ADVENTURE

THE CANADIAN AIRBORNE REGIMENT
1968-1995

he existence of both the Mobile Striking Force and the Defence of Canada Force was largely conceptual in nature. Neither of these two organizational entities ever represented a genuine operational capability. This state of affairs stemmed from the fact that very few individuals in the national military or political leadership believed that there was a credible role in Canada for paratroopers. Quite simply, Canadian airborne forces were seen as a diversion of already limited resources required for the more important North Atlantic Treaty Organization (NATO) and/or United Nations (UN) roles. The Defence of Canada task, specifically the requirement to parachute into remote hinterland to strike enemy lodgements, was viewed with contempt. Canadian military and political analysis consistently refuted the likelihood of a Soviet land invasion via the exposed northern flank. Moreover, as the threat became largely defined in terms of the manned bomber, the relevance of the paratrooper was further blurred.

General J.V. Allard and Colonel D.H. Rochester. *(Photographer unknown, CFPU CNL Neg. IE-69-191)*

General J.V. Allard, "Father" of the Canadian Airborne Regiment, inspects his paratroopers on 8 August 1969 during the first Regimental Change of Command Parade.
(Photographer unknown, CFPU CNL, Neg. IE-69-181.

Paratroopers preparing to commence an exercise with a ramp jump. *(R22R Archives)*

The final death knell for Canada's airborne soldiers was struck with the advent of the inter-continental ballistic missile (ICBM) in 1957. The military and scientific communities believed the ICBM threat to be virtually impervious to any defensive effort to stop it. The focus of military activity in the North subsequently shifted from active defence to surveillance. Consequently, the perception that the Arctic was a vulnerable flank, much less a gateway to invasion, underwent a rapid transformation. The North now became viewed as strategic depth. Militarily, it warranted limited attention and the barest of resources. Accordingly, paratroopers became the nation's insurance policy for its remote northern regions.

Prudent fiscal management necessitated that the cost be directly correlated to the level of peril. Since the risk was viewed as negligible, the lowest possible premium was deemed acceptable. This was not surprising. The tenuous existence of the country's paratroopers had long ago been strapped to the Guardians of the North concept. The idea of enemy lodgements on Canadian territory, as ethereal as it was, represented the only accepted rationale for maintaining airborne forces. But the reality had always been based on the premise no credible threat, no credible airborne organization. As a result, Canada's airborne capability was consistently marginalized.

Not surprisingly, this dictated that the state of military parachuting changed to a strictly survival mode. The skill was being kept alive, but just barely. Undeniably, the Army's focus was mechanized forces for NATO and the European battlefield. Paratroopers, who were perceived as costly and irrelevant, were not allowed to interfere with this paradigm. However, the government, specifically the Department of External Affairs, became increasingly interested in UN deployments. The UN intervention in the 1956 Suez Crisis through the use of an emergency force, created a growing Canadian interest and involvement.

The following year, Lester B. Pearson, the Canadian Secretary of State for External Affairs and the originator of the Suez Emergency Force concept, publicly asserted the necessity of countries earmarking small forces for UN duty to perform such functions as securing ceasefires agreed upon by belligerents. In January 1958, Canada officially designated a "Stand-By Battalion" for United Nations tasks. By the early sixties the notion of an Army rapid-reaction capability gathered further momentum. An unofficial announcement leaked from National Defence Headquarters hinted that a new defence policy, based on the concept of a small mobile airborne army with tactical air support, was beginning to take shape. Not surprisingly, the defence department's 1964 White Paper embodied a distinct new philosophy for the Canadian Armed Forces. The fortunes of the nation's paratroops appeared to be on the ascent.

Paul Hellyer, the Minister of Defence, intended the new defence document to provide a fresh blueprint for the next decade. "The purpose of our forces in being," stated Hellyer, "[was] to preserve peace by deterring war." He planned to achieve this by restructuring the military into a global and very mobile force which could meet the widest range of potential requirements in the quickest possible time. The theory postulated that rapid dispatch of these forces could contain conflict and prevent it from escalating into a more dangerous and less manageable crisis.

In 1966, Lieutenant-General Jean Victor Allard, the new commander of Force Mobile Command (FMC), explained to the Standing Committee of National Defence that the new Army organization was the result of a defence analysis which examined Canadian commitments and potential conditions of conflict. Allard described a scale of conflict ranging from peace and peacekeeping operations to limited and total war. He rationalized that different elements of the Army were seen as being better suited to respond to different circumstances along the scale. Hence, he believed, Mobile Command must be structured to provide an effective and capable response for the entire spectrum of conflict. He candidly confessed that at present the Canadian Army was designed primarily for only the upper end of the scale, namely a total global war. Consequently, he realized that it demonstrated great deficiencies for the lower range of activities such as peacekeeping, counter-insurgency, guerilla and limited warfare. Allard added that the anticipated range of potential confrontations, based on an Army appreciation, deduced that a "significant portion of the Canadian Army Field Force must be capable of operating in limited war in any part of the world."

The assessment resolved that the "Army must be strategically mobile and possess tactical mobility suitable to the scale of conflict and appropriate to the areas of operations." The report further declared that, in the final analysis, the Army's organization should be based on two basic types of formations and units. First, light airborne/air-transportable forces for the defence of the Canada-US region, peacekeeping, the Allied Command Europe (ACE) mobile force, and small limited wars; and secondly, heavier armoured and mechanized forces to fulfil the Canadian Army's role in NATO Europe. This conclusion was in consonance with Allard's proposal for the establishment of paratroops and light forces to deal with the type of conflict which could be expected at the lower end of the spectrum of conflict. Allard stressed strategic mobility. Specifically, he aimed to have a completely airportable unit, with all its equipment, deployed and in the designated operational theatre as quickly as forty-eight hours.

The mystery of how this would be achieved was quickly revealed.

On 12 May 1966, the minister of defence informed Parliament that "FMC would include the establishment of an airborne regiment whose personnel and equipment could be rapidly sent to danger zones." Undeniably, the future of the country's airborne soldiers was on the rise. Allard disclosed that this new organization would provide the flexibility the Army required. "We knew that the deployment of an infantry brigade overseas," he explained, "could take several weeks and even then only if it were already completely equipped and had received at least one month's thorough training." Allard added that "the light and rapid airborne regiment was meant to 'fill the bill' between the time the government acceded to a request for intervention from outside and the arrival of the main body of troops. This regiment was therefore designed to fill a gap in our strategy for modern warfare."

The concept of a Canadian airborne capability now escaped the narrow confines of the North and the restrictive defence of Canada role. Important is the fact that the Army Commander's vision was a direct result of his condemnation of the current organizational structure of the nation's paratroops, namely the DCF concept. An assessment conducted by his headquarters staff revealed that the "dispersal of parachutists in small operational and training packets leads to a loss of overall airborne effectiveness and efficiency." Furthermore, the report concluded, it violated the principle of economy by duplication of training facilities and other functions, as well as causing unnecessary disruption and resultant inefficiency to three battalions, at any one time, and in the long term, forced unwanted organizational changes on half the infantry corps. The study clearly recommended that "every effort must be made to concentrate all airborne operational and training resources in the one unit." Of equal importance was Lieutenant-General Allard's emphasis on the training value of the envisioned airborne unit. The Army Commander clearly conveyed this notion to the Parliamentary Committee on Defence. Allard felt that "this light unit is going to be very attractive to a fellow who likes to live dangerously, so all volunteers can go into it." His creation was to be open to all three services and manned exclusively by volunteers. "We intend," he asserted, "to look at the individual a little more rather than considering the unit as a large body of troops, some of whom might not be suited for the task."

Allard heralded the commencement of a new chapter in the history of Canada's airborne forces. As a result, justifiably, Lieutenant-General Jean Victor Allard considered himself the father of the Canadian Airborne Regiment (Cdn AB Regt). By early 1966, the MSF/DCF model of decentralized parachute capability was soundly condemned. The official FMC assessment on the airborne requirement in the Canadian Army clearly specified that "quick reaction and the ability to undertake operations virtually anywhere in the world over a wide range of climatic, terrain and operational conditions are essential ingredients of the airborne force." It categorically confirmed that for reasons of maximum effectiveness, efficiency and economy in a field force with a strictly limited manpower budget, the most suitable method of meeting the parachutist requirement was to form a permanent airborne regiment consisting of two small battalions with appropriate support arms.

Amazingly, in an environment of shrinking military resources, the parachute capability actually expanded. In the spring of 1966, General Allard, now the Chief of the Defence Staff (CDS), took the next step and discussed

Paratrooper displaying good landing form. *(R22R Archives)*

Paratrooper versus the environment. *(R22R Archives)*

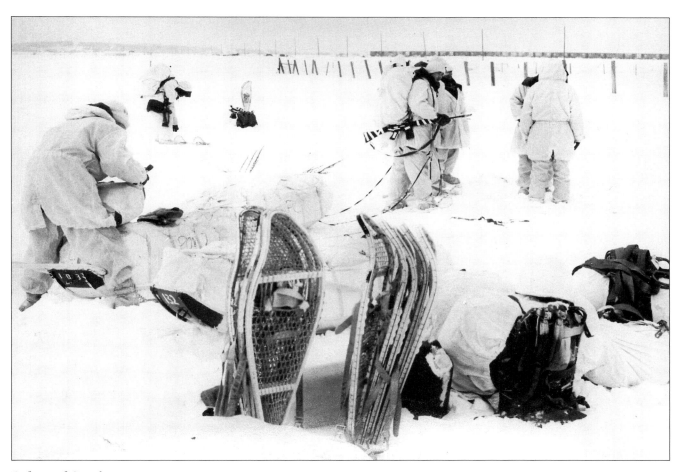

Defence of Canada. *(R22R Archives)*

Members of 1 Cdo exit a "Voyageur" helicopter after a security mission during Operation Essay, during the FLQ Crisis in Montreal, Quebec, October 1970.

(Cpl Johnson, CFPU CNL, Neg. IM-70-226)

Airborne soldiers rehearsing crowd control drills during the FLQ Crisis, October 1970.　　　　*(CAFM)*

the formation of the new "Airborne Commando Regiment" with Colonel Don H. Rochester. Less than a year later, Allard invited Rochester to Ottawa and appointed him the commander-designate of the embryonic organization. The new regimental commander was now given a further year to refine the "Concept of Operations," organization, and structure. The prospects seemed unlimited. The "exciting thing about General Allard's concept," recalled Rochester, "was that this unit was to be radically different. Except for aircraft, it was to be self-contained with infantry, armour, artillery, engineers, signals and supporting administration." Furthermore, he reminisced, "all were to be volunteers and so well trained in their own arm or service that they could devote their time to specialist training."

Colonel Rochester and his planning staff quickly began to work out the details concerning organization, strength, training requirements and unit location. Externally imposed changes began early in the administrative and planning process. A centrally directed manpower reduction scaled the regiment down from the original 1,285 positions to 898. This entailed the elimination of the proposed armoured squadron, as well as personnel cuts to the remaining units.

A further alteration affected the actual name of the organization. The senior military leadership decided that the word Commando in the title was too "aggressive." Consequently, the offensive word was dropped. However, this provided the solution to another quandary. The infantry components of the regiment were referred to as battalions, although they were far too small for this designation, but too large to be labelled as companies. As a result, the deleted term was quickly adopted for the infantry components which were subsequently called Commandos.

The location of the regiment was the next major question that Rochester's staff addressed. Possible military bases included Comox, Edmonton, Penhold, Petawawa, Picton, Rivers, Valcartier, and Wainwright. After exhaustive analysis and study, Edmonton was chosen because of its excellent air facilities and abundant drop zones; its important strategic location from a global vantage point; proximity to training areas at Wainwright, nearness to mountains and ski areas; and particularly because the

PPCLI was to move to Calgary, and the accommodation they were vacating was a custom fit.

Finally, on 8 April 1968, the Canadian Airborne Regiment was officially established. It consisted of an airborne headquarters and signal squadron, two infantry commandos, an airborne field battery and an airborne field squadron. By June the Regiment began to assemble in Griesbach Barracks, with the exception of 1 Commando which remained in CFB Valcartier for the interim. This delay was intended to provide time for the necessary francophone infrastructure, such as schools, to be established in Edmonton.

The Regiment's mandate was impressive. Lieutenant-General W.A.B. Anderson, the FMC Commander, dictated that the Cdn AB Regt was to be capable of performing a variety of tasks which included: the defence of Canada; the UN stand-by role; peacekeeping operations; missions in connection with national disaster; Special Air Service (SAS)-type missions; coup de main tasks in a general war setting; and responsibility for parachute training in the Canadian Forces.

The respective Canadian Forces Organizational Order (CFOO) stated that "the role of the Canadian Airborne Regiment is to provide a force capable of moving quickly to meet any unexpected enemy threat or other commitment of the Canadian Armed Forces." The nation's paratroopers, who had existed on the Army's periphery for their entire existence, were now touted as Canada's "fire-brigade." They became the country's vanguard force responsible for dispatching, within two days of a request being received, the first elements of a Canadian UN peacekeeping force.

The Guardians of the North were now established as a national strategic force for global employment. Colonel Rochester captured the essence of the excitement felt by all members of the new organization. He addressed his new command with the prophetic words, "ahead lies the great adventure of this new Regiment." He had reason to be optimistic.

The Regiment, as intended by General Allard, took only volunteers and was designed specifically for intrepid individuals. The type of soldiers expected to flock to the Regiment prompted Rochester to postulate that the new members "would be so dedicated to their cause, that normal disciplinary measures would not be needed."

The quality of the original individuals was in fact incontestable. Official recruiting themes stressed the superior attributes of the new genre of airborne warrior. They emphasised the fact that the paratrooper had to be an excellent athlete, an expert at small arms and a survival specialist. Furthermore, they underscored the necessity to be robust, courageous, and capable of a high level of endurance.

It was quickly realized that the Cdn AB Regt received a larger percentage of the more ambitious, determined and energized individuals. Frankly, they skimmed the cream of the Army. This was not surprising. Only experienced officers, non-commissioned officers, and soldiers were accepted. All riflemen within the commandos were required to be qualified to the rank of corporal. This meant that the respective individual had previously served within a regular rifle battalion. As a result, they were already competent and experienced in the basic drills of soldiering. Equally important, they were on the whole older and normally, more mature. This allowed the Regiment to direct its training effort towards specialized training such as mountain and pathfinder operations, patrolling courses, skiing, and unarmed combat.

The Cdn AB Regt quickly forged a reputation for undertaking tough, demanding and dynamic activities. It set new standards for physical fitness and training realism. Specifically, it revolutionized the manner in which the infantry conducted live fire exercises and firing ranges. In consonance with its status as a strategic force capable of global deployment, the Regiment travelled throughout Canada and the United States, as well as to exotic locations such as Jamaica to practise its lethal craft. By the early seventies the Airborne Regiment was at its zenith of power. It had the status of a mini-formation, direct access to the Commander of the Army, and a peacetime establishment of 1,044. Brigadier-General R.G. Therriault, the new Regimental Commander, acknowledged that the Regiment was favoured. He explained that "[we] had greater training opportunities; no summer taskings or commitments to the Reserves; and free reign to do our own thing." Therriault candidly

conceded that in the early years, the Airborne Regiment "was given more, and other people didn't like it."

The first major organizational change occurred in June 1970. A mechanized infantry battalion stationed in Baden-Soellingen, Germany, was added to the Canadian Airborne Regiment's Order of Battle. The unit, designated 3 Mechanized Commando, wore the maroon beret despite the fact that a large number of its members were not jump-qualified, nor did the unit have a jump role. Furthermore, it never exercised in conjunction with the rest of the Regiment.

To the paratroopers serving in Canada, 3 Mechanized Commando was an anomaly that should never have been directly associated with the Canadian Airborne Regiment. The stark reality was a bureaucratic marriage of convenience. The new unit was a RCR/PPCLI hybrid which had resulted from the 1969/1970 FMC reorganization. The old Army structure had contained eleven infantry battalions, as well as the Cdn AB Regt with two rifle commandos. The re-organization cut several regiments but established three battalions for each of the RCR, PPCLI and R22eR infantry regiments. However, the existence in the Canadian Army Order of Battle of a tenth battalion required a solution which did not necessitate the establishment of a new regiment, but allowed for the retention of the balance between the surviving infantry regiments. Conveniently, 3 Mechanized Commando was formed. This created a new Army structure consisting of 9 infantry battalions and the Cdn AB Regt consisting of two rifle commandos and a mechanized battalion. It was strictly an expedient solution to a potentially awkward situation. The vast separation, both doctrinally and geographically, between the paratroopers in Canada and the mechanized troops of 3 Mechanized Commando in Europe, ensured that the two entities continued to lead their own separate identities.

The Regiment's first operational test came in the fall of 1970 during the FLQ Crisis in Quebec. On 15 October 1970, the Quebec provincial government officially solicited the assistance of the armed forces in aid of the civil power, citing the need to "help the police protect the public and public buildings." The request was received in Ottawa at 1250 hours, and within forty minutes two aircraft carrying the lead elements of the

1 Cdo deploying for Ex Grand Désert, Ancienne Lorette, Quebec, 1968.
(R22R Archives)

Canadian Airborne Regiment departed Namao Airfield in Edmonton to begin the Regiment's participation in Operation (OP) Essay.

The Regiment set up its temporary quarters at St.-Hubert Airfield with smaller detachments located around Camp Farnham, Camp Bouchard, St. Sauver and Sorel. It was organized into four rapid-reaction teams. These Airborne groups were tasked with assisting the municipal and provincial police forces in the conduct of sweeps, raids and other internal security missions. Each quick response element was given a specific niche. One team was code-named Eagle and assigned as the Regiment's heliborne force. Another group was titled, Speed due to its reliance on wheeled transport, and a third team was denoted Stand-By; ready to move anywhere, anytime, anyhow. The fourth and final organization was the Reserve Force. Their responsibility was to rotate tasks with the other groups to ensure all had an adequate ability to rest. The tension and sense of crisis began to dissipate by early November and the Regiment returned to Edmonton on the seventeenth of that month.

Overall, the Canadian Armed Forces' participation in OP Essay totalled approximately ten thousand personnel and was officially terminated on 4 January 1971.

The Airborne's next operational test came less than four years later. It began in April 1974 with the rotation of 1 Commando to the idyllic Mediterranean island of Cyprus as part of the Canadian commitment to the United Nations Force in Cyprus (UNFICYP). Considerable unrest on the island, foreshadowing the crisis that would soon occur, was apparent during the early part of the tour.

On the morning of 15 July, UNFICYP was put on general alert. Violent fire fights between Cypriot forces raged throughout the city. By noon it became apparent that the Greek Cypriot National Guard was in complete control of Nicosia, the capital city, as well as of the Cypriot government. The guard had staged a coup d'etat and deposed the president, Archbishop Makarios III.

Amazingly, the coup came as a complete surprise to UNFICYP.

Five days later the crisis escalated. During the dead of night, the Canadian contingent was notified by UNFICYP Headquarters that a Turkish invasion was imminent. The expected assault began later that morning. The Turkish government decided to intervene, justifying its action on the premise that it had an obligation to safeguard the rights of the Turkish Cypriot minority. As a result, the Turks conducted parachute drops and amphibious operations which soon established a corridor from Nicosia in the heart of the island, to Kyrenia on the sea. It later became apparent that this was only the first phase of the plan.

As the onslaught progressed it became necessary to evacuate UN Observation Posts because of direct and indirect fire. To make matters worse, the Greek National Guard utilized UN positions to shield its own activities, particularly the firing of mortars.

Despite continuing efforts by the UN forces, it proved impossible to negotiate an armistice during the first day of the invasion. By 24 July, the situation stabilized and a ceasefire took hold, but it was not to last. The temporary lull, however, enabled the deployment of the bulk of the

Heavily laden paratroopers from 1 Cdo en route to the objective. *(R22R Archives)*

Airborne Regiment to augment the Canadian contingent, including 1 Commando. The Airborne Regimental Commander, Colonel G.H. Lessard, subsequently assumed command on 2 August.

Now that the contingent was reinforced by additional personnel and Armoured Personnel Carriers (APCs), it began to flex its muscle and insist on freedom of movement. On numerous occasions roadblocks put up by Turkish forces and the Greek National Guard were forcibly removed. In addition, more observation posts were established and the entirety of no-man's land was heavily patrolled.

By mid August, UNFICYP was again put on heightened alert, and at dawn on 14 August the second phase of the Turkish offensive began. Both sides quickly began to deliberately target the UN. As a result, by 0812 hours, the last of the Canadian positions were evacuated. In the next few days observation posts would be manned and evacuated as necessitated by events. Ceasefires were attempted but repeatedly failed. Throughout the offensive, the paratroopers and their vehicles were consistently targeted and engaged by both small arms and mortar fire.

Two days later, with their objectives secured, the Turks implemented a unilateral ceasefire. Nevertheless, the situation remained tense as both sides uneasily settled into defensive positions. Despite the cessation of hostilities the environment remained dangerous.

Throughout this period a firm, resolute stand by the Canadian paratroopers maintained the integrity of the buffer zone. The Regiment undertook the task of establishing and enforcing the demarcation line, providing organization and security for prisoner of war (PoW) exchanges; and providing escorts for infrastructure repair. The Canadian troops also assisted twenty thousand refugees. The paratroopers delivered tons of food and supplies, including blankets, cots and tents, prior to the arrival of the International Committee of the Red Cross (ICRC) and other humanitarian agencies.

For their efforts, the airborne soldiers earned two Stars of Courage and six Medals of Bravery. However, a great price was paid for these honours. In the brief period the Regiment was engaged in this conflict, it suffered thirty casualties, including two dead.

Upon the Regiment's return to Canada, it once again commenced its demanding training cycle. But, in less than two years, the Airborne found itself deployed on operations for the third time within its first decade of service. During the first week of July 1976, the Regiment deployed on OP Gamescan, the designation given to the Canadian Forces security operation at the 1976 Montreal Olympics. The bulk of the Regiment was stationed at the Collège militaire royal de St-Jean. Given the designation of Task Force III, the Airborne once again found itself performing the role of a quick-reaction force, and was able to demonstrate its expertise and versatility. Fortunately, it was never called upon to react to a genuine crisis. The operation was a success and no incident similar to the catastrophe suffered at the Munich Olympics four years previously was experienced.

Continuation parachute drops onto DZ Buxton, Edmonton, Alberta. Continuation parachute descents were specifically conducted to maintain jumper currency. In accordance with CF regulations every parachutist is required to jump once every three months or the individual is obligated to undergo refresher training prior to parachuting. *(Don Halcrow)*

The DZ was named after RSM Richard G. Buxton who died when his parachute failed to open during a free fall jump on 30 July 1971. *(CAFM)*

111

Unbeknownst to the Regiment at the time, the Canadian Airborne had reached its apex. Continual budgetary pressures were slowly eroding the Canadian Armed Forces' resources and strength. Predictably, the effects began to chip away at the nation's airborne capability as well.

In December 1974, the Cabinet had authorized the initiation of a Defence Structure Review. General Jacques Dextraze, the CDS and a prominent committee member, quickly announced that "hard operational needs would determine the basic structuring of the forces." It was clear that only those organizations which had a pervasive and undisputable role to fill could breathe easy.

Ominously, the "airborne family" recognized that Dextraze was anything but a supporter of paratroops. The CDS perceived parachute soldiers as costly and redundant. He even dismissed their importance as "protectors of the North." Dextraze rejected the notion of an Arctic threat and preferred to exercise sovereignty in that area with a more tangible presence, such as an organization centred on people who resided in the region, and who would perform patrolling and surveillance duties. He hypothesized that this force would be supported by the Northern Region Headquarters, Canadian Forces airbases, and a new training facility on Devon Island. Dextraze clearly announced that he did not believe that paratroops were an economical or effective tool for the task.

Not surprisingly, in late December 1975, he briefed a gathering in Montreal that one of the units considered for disbandment or removal as part of the ongoing defence structure review was the Canadian Airborne Regiment in Edmonton. The CDS later publicly declared that he could not afford to have any one formation of the Canadian Forces become unduly specialized. Dextraze's perception of the Airborne's role was one of simply assisting every other formation and the Government of Canada in any missions the Canadian Forces may be given. He did not ascribe to them any special responsibility or status.

The initial musings of disbandment fomented a storm of resistance. General Dextraze now deftly appeared to take a new approach. A year following his first trial balloon, the CDS addressed the Conference of Defence Associates in Ottawa. In this forum he confided, "My two major problems with the current army posture are that it could be better balanced geographically, and that I do not have enough people to fill the sharp end vacancies which exist." Dextraze then opined that he could correct these problems by relocating the Cdn AB Regt and subordinating it to another formation. He explained that the Army would then have three, rather than four, major army formations in Canada, each with integral supporting arms and services.

General Dextraze painted a further "hypothetical scenario" for the assembled audience. He visualized the establishment of a highly mobile, rapid-reaction formation stationed in the centre of Canada, with its headquarters in CFB Petawawa. The CDS outlined that the organization would consist of an air-landed battalion and a major airborne unit formed from the current Cdn AB Regt in which there would be an RCR, a PPCLI, and a R22eR commando. Dextraze subsequently directed FMC Headquarters to study and prepare a plan for the reorganization and relocation of the Army in Canada along these lines.

Increasingly, resistance mounted. Internal studies conflicted with Dextraze's assertion that the Regiment would be more operationally effective in Ontario. In addition, opposition from outside the military also grew. Alberta politicians, concerned with the economic impact of the move, created much discomfort for the CDS. To exacerbate the situation, a protest movement called the "Save the Regiment Committee," composed of former serving members and concerned citizens and widely supported by the Royal Canadian Legion membership, began an active campaign to lobby both the provincial and federal governments. The committee went so far as to write a letter to Her Majesty, Queen Elizabeth II asking her to intercede on behalf of the Canadian Airborne Regiment.

Nonetheless, on 26 November 1976, the decision to move the Regiment to Petawawa was formally authorized by Cabinet. In the wake of this verdict, Dextraze clearly announced that the decision was strictly a military one. He stated, "the plan comes from me, I made it." The CDS fervently defended his actions. Almost a year to the day after his initial musing to the Conference of Defence Associates, Dextraze briefed them once again on his final design. He explained that he had decided on a peacetime establishment based on a standard brigade group in the west, a standard brigade group in the east and a force of regimental size in the centre, which he tentatively designated the "Special Service Force" (SSF). He elaborated that the SSF was slightly different and provided the Army with a relatively light, airborne/airportable quick-reaction force in the demographic centre of the country which could be moved quickly to augment either of the flanking brigades for internal security tasks, to the Arctic, or to UN-type operations.

The move and reorganization became a defining moment for the Canadian Airborne Regiment. It signalled nothing short of the organization's eventual demise.

Of prime importance, and instrumental to the Regiment's subsequent decline, was the loss of independent formation status. It was now simply an integral part of the newly created Special Service Force. The Cdn AB Regt became nothing more than just another infantry unit, albeit an airborne one. It lost its special exemption from taskings and was now given assignments in the same manner as the other units within the SSF.

However, there was a more serious consequence. As the Regiment became defined and viewed as just another infantry unit, its claim on seasoned officers and soldiers was dismissed. Tragically, it lost its preferred manning. It was no longer in the enviable position of receiving only experienced and mature leaders and men. Prior to the reorganization all riflemen within the commandos had to be qualified to the rank of corporal. This of course meant that those soldiers were generally more mature and experienced. However, after the move to CFB Petawawa, this prerequisite no longer existed. The resultant influx of younger, less mature and junior soldiers soon transformed the very character of the Airborne.

The restructuring inflicted additional wounds. The Regiment was dramatically pared. Its integral airborne engineer squadron and airborne artillery battery were removed from the Order of Battle. The requirement to fulfill those capabilities fell to 2 Combat Engineer Regiment and "E" Battery, 2 Royal Canadian Horse Artillery, within the SSF. Both these units were responsi-

ble for providing airborne-qualified personnel and equipment in support, when required, to the Canadian Airborne Regiment. In turn, the Regiment, once so configured, became designated as the Canadian Airborne Regiment Battle Group. Additionally, the Airborne Service Support Unit was also disbanded. First-line service support was provided by the newly formed 1 Airborne Service Support Company, and second-line support by 2 Service Battalion, which was another unit within the SSF. Also stricken from the Order of Battle was 3 Mechanized Commando. Personnel serving in this unit were returned to Canada and subsequently re-badged to form 3 RCR, newly established in Petawawa. As part of the reorganization, a third rifle commando, designated 3 Airborne Commando was authorized, but not yet organized or manned.

Operational effectiveness was also degraded. In Edmonton, the Cdn AB Regt was located in tandem with the Canadian Airborne [Training] Centre (CABC), and the Airborne Maintenance Depot, which was responsible for parachute packing and maintenance. Furthermore, the paratroopers were co-located with a first-class all-weather air base, which was soundly situated from a strategic viewpoint for access to the Canadian North or the world. The air base was also the home for two air transport squadrons, one of which was directly tasked to provide the airborne forces with their tactical mobility and essential training support. Critical to airborne operations was the fact that both the respective land and air components, which together comprised the nation's strategic airborne capability, were located together in this one location. This all vanished with the move. A Commission of Inquiry later concluded that "the reorganization had the effect of diluting the CAR's [Canadian Airborne Regiment's] former uniqueness in the army."

Despite the reduction in size and loss of operational effectiveness, the reorganization entailed two additional new tasks. The first was the nebulous requirement to provide a quick-response airborne capability as part of the national rescue plan in the event of a major air disaster (MAJAID). The second added function was the necessity for the Regiment to be capable of acting as a Cyprus commitment rotation unit. The latter task quickly raised

Above and facing page: Entry by another means. Paratroopers use assault boats to conduct beach assault and jungle training in Jamaica, during Ex Nimrod Caper IV, April 1972.

(MCpl Johnson, CFPU CNL, Neg. REC 72-92)

(MCpl Johnson, CFPU CNL, Neg. REC 72-169)

(MCpl Johnson, CFPU CNL, Neg. REC 72-174)

concern about the Airborne's continuing suitability to act as a national strategic reserve or UN stand-by force, if in fact it was committed to a lengthy six- to nine-month assignment. The quandary was never resolved or actually seriously addressed. Multiple taskings were accepted as a necessary evil in an environment with an acknowledged "capability/commitment gap."

The normal hectic training cycle was quickly resumed in Petawawa. Nevertheless, a certain degree of discontent and seething resentment was still present by the summer of 1978 when yet another tempest swept through the Airborne. Still reeling from its dramatic degeneration, the Regiment's utility, as well as its existence, was once again questioned. Barney Danson, the Minister of National Defence, launched the latest assault with an inference to the media that the Regiment might be disbanded. The ensuing controversy prompted a clarification, at which time he declared that "Canada cannot afford the luxury of an unassigned unit to be inactive." Another press account attributed to the MND the statement that "an elite unit, with no assigned tasks, seems out of place today." The latest attack on the Regiment prompted Colonel J.J. Painchaud, the well-respected and outspoken Regimental Commander, to publicly criticize the minister. Audaciously, Painchaud demanded that Danson be replaced if he did not stop such "irresponsible" statements. Not surprisingly, Painchaud was swiftly reassigned.

The final manifestation of the 1977-78 reorganization also took effect at this time. In June 1979, 3 Airborne Commando was officially established as the third rifle commando within the Canadian Airborne Regiment. The Regiment's infantry units were now organized in such a manner that each of the three commandos became affiliated with their parent infantry regiment. For example, 1, 2, and 3 Airborne Commandos were manned by officers and soldiers of the R22eR, PPCLI, and RCR, respectively. The senior Army leadership believed the initiative would solve the Regiment's chronic manpower shortages. They explained that each parent infantry regiment had a quota to fill to meet the requirements of its respective commando. Shortfalls, the senior commanders added, would be highly visible and easily attributable to the source.

Another motive which prompted the move to specifically aligned commandos was a belief that affiliating commandos to a parent organization would create within the feeder infantry regiments, a distinct pride. The Army leadership argued that this would ensure that these regiments would send only their best personnel to the Canadian Airborne Regiment. This notion would later prove to be rather naive.

With the commencement of a new decade, Edmonton had become a memory and the paratroopers settled into their new home. In 1981, the Regiment returned to Cyprus, this time under more tranquil circumstances, as the thirty-fifth Canadian peacekeeping rotation to UNFICYP. The tour was routine and uneventful. Upon the Regiment's return to Canada the soldiers resumed their trademark pace of challenging and demanding training.

In the spring of 1983, the Regiment reaped a windfall as a result of a program under which militia units were tasked to provide integral, operationally-ready sub-units for the defence of Canada. Consequently, the Cdn AB Regt became distinctly linked to three militia Regiments: Le Régiment du Saguenay (R du Sag), the Loyal Edmonton Regiment (L Edmn R), and the Queen's Own Rifles of Canada (QOR of C). FMC tasked each of these militia units with the responsibility of providing an airborne platoon to augment 1, 2, and 3 Airborne Commandos respectively with trained parachutists for reinforcement in the case of an emergency. Two years later, the airborne tasking was expanded. The Royal Westminster Regiment (R Westmr R) was now added to the family. It was responsible for supplying, on order, an airborne platoon to reinforce 2 Airborne Commando. In addition, the existing tasking to the other militia units was also enlarged. The "Total Force" concept now provided a potentially significant addition to the Airborne.

The Militia augmentation represented a total of two operationally tasked company headquarters (QOR of C and R du Sag) and six platoons broken down as follows: two from QOR of C, two from R du Sag, one from the L Edmn R, and one from the R Westmr R. In times of crisis the Airborne Regiment could now add a fourth rifle platoon to its rifle commandos by incorporating the three Militia platoons. Furthermore, the remaining Militia

Winter exercise drop in Dundurn, Saskatchewan. *(Don Halcrow)*

Paratroopers participating in the Regimental Ski School at Kanananaskis, Alberta, 27 January 1972.

(Webb, CFPU CNL, Neg. IE-72-10)

Winter exercise in Grays Flat, Alberta, 1973. *(Don Halcrow)*

Paratroopers fire the backbone of the airborne arsenal, the .30 calibre General Purpose Machine Gun. *(CAFM)*

Mock Tower exit by the McLean brothers, CFB Edmonton, 8 April 1969. *(Stevens, CFPU CNL, Neg. IE 69-66)*

Parachute Maintenance Depot, CFB Edmonton. *(Photographer unknown, CFPU CNL, Neg. PCN 74-730)*

Middle and bottom: An airborne staple — unarmed combat. *(CAFM)*

Regardless of time or place, the Mock Tower maintains its dreaded role. *(CAFM)*

118

platoons and a composite Militia company headquarters could also form the nucleus of a fourth commando.

Despite the positive step in augmentation and the eventual integration into the SSF, by the mid eighties a disturbing problem became evident within the Regiment. A large number of highly visible criminal incidents, some involving members of the Regiment, raised the concern of senior Army leaders that in the SSF, particularly in the Canadian Airborne Regiment, an abnormally high incidence of anti-social behaviour, such as assaults, weapon thefts, and substance abuse was prevalent. Continuing serious disciplinary transgressions and a highly publicized killing committed by a paratrooper from 1 Airborne Commando in the summer of 1985 brought the crisis to a head. The machete murder of a civilian in Fort Coulonge, Quebec, mere weeks after a rash of weapon thefts, pushed the crisis to the brink.

In anger over this incident, the CDS perfunctorily ordered the disbandment of the Regiment. Fortunately for the Canadian Airborne Regiment, the Acting Army Commander, Major-General Jean de Chastelain, was able to calm the situation and offer a compromise solution. As a result, the Chief of Defence Staff agreed to the commission of an investigation designated the *FMC Study on Disciplinary Infractions and Antisocial Behaviour within FMC with Particular Reference to the Special Service Force and the Canadian Airborne Regiment*. This probe became known informally as the Hewson Report. Its aim was to review disciplinary infractions within FMC and investigate the determinants which led to the excessive antisocial behaviour.

The report was tabled in September 1985 and concluded that there was in fact a higher number of assault cases in the Airborne Regiment compared to the other infantry units in the Army. The study team attributed the discrepancy in behaviour to a combination of factors, such as: the absence of junior leaders; the immaturity and lack of experience of some of the replacements sent to the Cdn AB Regt; and the semi-isolation of CFB Petawawa itself, which failed to provide an adequate number of drinking establishments and other off-base social outlets which could absorb the large single male population of the base. The study team further noted that

there was a need to base selection of junior leaders for service with the Airborne on the particular demand for mature, capable leaders with good common sense. It also added that previous experience in a regular infantry battalion should be, once again, a prerequisite for all volunteers.

Nonetheless, the assessment clearly stated, "there is no cause for alarm or requirement for precipitate action." It went on to argue that there appeared to be a lower incidence of serious pathology and violent behaviour in the Canadian Forces than in the Canadian population at large.

The report quickly became inconsequential. Under the tutelage of Colonel J.M.R. Gaudreau, the new and well-respected Regimental Commander, the chaotic state of discipline appeared to ameliorate. Gaudreau believed that the answer to the disciplinary problems lay in the tenets of good solid soldiering, namely firm discipline and hard challenging training. He candidly explained, "these problems after all, although serious in nature, had been experienced in all other Combat Arms units in the past at one time or another." In the final analysis, the Hewson Report had no impact on the Cdn AB Regt. Despite the momentary scrutiny, the rapid pace of airborne soldiering raged on for the paratroopers. The Regiment continued to focus its efforts in the late eighties on the UN Ready Force and defence of Canada roles.

Major activities included Exercise Nimrod Caper in Fort Bliss, Texas, in 1985. This deployment was designed to rehearse the Canadian Airborne Regiment Battle Group, as the UN Immediate Reaction Force, at deployment and stability operations within a UN context. During this period the Regiment was also heavily involved in the SSF-controlled Exercise Lightning Strike series which focussed on the DCO role. In addition, the Regiment was also called upon to conduct another UNFICYP rotation in the fall of 1986. Although the tour was uneventful, the Regiment did take the opportunity to maximize its proximity to the British Parachute Regiment, which was also serving in Cyprus. Unit exchanges and joint training were undertaken. The occasion, true to the renown airborne initiative, was fully exploited. Prior to the tour's termination both Regiments became officially affiliated.

Drop into the Mojave Desert, California, September 1973. *(Don Halcrow)*

A paratrooper monitors the Alaskan Highway from his mountain observation post, south of Whitehorse, Yukon. *(Don Halcrow)*

Defence of the North. Regimental exercise in Resolute Bay, NWT, 1973. *(Don Halcrow)*

In spite of a very active training regimen, the Canadian Airborne Regiment commenced its third decade as a malcontent organization. Despite the historic labelling of the paratroopers the nation's Quick Reaction Force and the designated UN Stand-By Force, the reality was very much different. With the exception of the emergency deployment to Cyprus in 1974, the Airborne was never employed in an operational capacity other than normal Cyprus rotation tours. Of great distress to Canada's pre-eminent combat troops was the reality that rather than deploying to "hot spots" throughout the globe, the paratroopers were instead used to train others to proceed overseas on actual operations. This relegated Canada's airborne soldiers to a position on the sidelines as trainers instead of warriors. The Regiment assisted in the preparation to deploy communication and service support units to Iran/Iraq and Namibia. They provided support and watched as the SSF deployed elements of 1 RCR and 2 Field Ambulance for the Gulf War. But the final humiliation came in the torpid summer heat of 1990. Mohawks, angered over a municipal decision to convert into a golf course local land they considered sacred but whose ownership was disputed, turned to violence to halt construction. On 17 August, after a month-long standoff between Mohawk Natives and law enforcement officers, the Quebec government asked the Canadian Forces to replace the provincial police at the barricades of Oka. Ten days later the provincial government submitted a further request to dismantle the Mohawk barriers. Elements of both the SSF and 5 CMBG were swiftly deployed. The Commander of the Army also gave the Canadian Airborne Regiment a mandate to prepare for possible deployment to Oka.

Lieutenant-General Kent Foster considered the paratroopers his "ace in the hole." As a result, six weeks of diligent training was undertaken. Mock-ups of the barricades were constructed and the paratroopers exercised every conceivable contingency. However, when the crisis ended on 26 September, the Regiment had never even left Petawawa.

Time is the ultimate healer and the latest disappointment eventually faded away. Key to this process was the prospect of an upcoming operation that quickly sparked renewed excitement and optimism. In mid July 1991,

Marcel Masse, the Minister of National Defence, announced that Canada was contributing 740 troops to participate in the United Nations Mission for the Referendum in Western Sahara. Of primary significance was the fact that the contribution for the new mission, designated OP Python, was based on the Canadian Airborne Regiment. The mandate assigned the paratroopers the role of monitoring a proposed ceasefire and ensuring that troop reductions and prisoner of war (PoW) exchanges, which were mutually agreed to by POLISARIO guerillas and the Moroccan army, were honoured. Training for the deployment began on 1 September. The Regiment was to be in position in the Western Sahara by the beginning of November. The preparatory work-ups were quickly completed. Vehicles were painted and packed. Equipment was diligently readied and crated. Ominously, dates began to slip. Postponements were followed by further delays. Not surprisingly, "on again-off again" direction became rampant, and the operation was quickly dubbed OP "Monty" Python. By December, even the diehard optimists realized the mission was a bust. The operation never materialized. The two warring factions failed to resolve the issue of who was qualified to vote in the referendum. Consequently the proposed UN mission collapsed and the focus of the international body became one of simply trying to sustain the existing observers in place.

This latest disappointment fuelled the already boiling cauldron of disillusionment. Major-General J.M.R. Gaudreau candidly acknowledged that the state of affairs was "a real bone of contention for all ranks of the Regiment who were on 'stand-by' for everything, yet saw conventional units getting the tasks." The circumstances of the latest setback did little to allay resentment.

The absence of an operational mission was not the Regiment's only immediate pressing concern. Continuing budgetary restraints in the Canadian Forces resulted in yet another reorganization being imposed on the Canadian Airborne Regiment. Concurrent with the preparations for the ill-fated OP Python was an announcement which directed that the Regiment be officially reduced from regimental to battalion status. The new structure took effect on 24 June 1992, and coincided with the change of command from Colonel W.M.

Airborne "armour." The anomaly of 3 Mechanized Commando in Europe. *(CAFM)*

Holmes to Lieutenant-Colonel P.R. Morneault. The reorganization reduced the Regiment from a strength of 754 members down to a paltry 601 all ranks.

Surprisingly, in spite of the reduction of strength and resources, this latest change had no effect on the Regiment's official role. Incredibly, the paratroopers maintained their all-inclusive mission statement. The new restructured "airborne battalion" retained the identical role and tasks given in the 1977 and revised 1985 Canadian Forces Organizational Order, namely, to "provide rapid deployment of airborne/air-transportable forces capable of responding to any emergency situation in support of national security or international peacekeeping." This state of affairs prompted repeated warnings

from both the SSF and Regimental commanders, as well as other staff officers. Some feared that the assigned taskings across such a broad spectrum of conflict required an organization greater than that of a battalion. However, the necessary level of actual capability was assessed against probable threat. The fact that the airborne soldiers had never been deployed on a mission or within a time-frame that could not be matched by a more conventional unit made the potential risk of a scaled-down airborne organization acceptable.

The Airborne did manage one small but significant victory. Despite the regression to battalion status, the airborne unit was authorized to retain the designation Canadian Airborne Regiment. The motive for the retention of the title, nonetheless, lay more in economy than in concern over tradition. It was quickly realized that a significant investment in regimental accoutrements, associations, clothing, kit shops, messes, and museums, was not something cheaply tampered with.

Amazingly, the reorganization had little effect on the rank and file. To the paratroopers within the rifle commandos little seemed to change. Training remained constant: challenging, demanding, and hectic. Issues relating to command ranks, legalities concerning reduced authority and powers of punishments, and the nuances of new titles were irrelevant to the soldiers and junior officers. Moreover, their primary focus was on what was believed to be a potential deployment to the Western Sahara. Unfortunately, as already indicated, this failed to transpire.

Understandably, the Regiment's third decade of service quickly became one of despondency. Reduced in size and status, the paratroopers also felt the sting of missed operational deployments. The dispatch of mechanized forces to the former Yugoslavia only heightened the sense of impotence which began to permeate the ranks. But the winds began to shift.

The summer of 1992 sparked a chain of events which would dramatically change the fortunes of Canada's airborne warriors. At this time, the UN secretary-general called for an enlarged UN presence in the strife-torn country of Somalia. The proposed force was to include military observers as well as an armed security force. The secretary-general's request was unanimously accepted by the Security Council and on 27 July 1992, UN Security Council Resolution 767, calling for the secretary-general and the international community to provide urgent humanitarian assistance to Somalia, was passed.

Within two weeks Canada advised the UN that it was willing to provide transport aircraft to deliver humanitarian relief supplies. More importantly, the prime minister acknowledged that Canada was prepared to contribute a contingent of security troops within the context of a larger UN force. This offer was quickly accepted. On 25 August an informal request was passed to Canada asking for the provision of a self-contained battalion to participate in the mission in the Horn of Africa. Eight days later, the Minister of National Defence announced that

Canada was deploying 750 peacekeepers as part of a classical UN peacekeeping operation mandated under Chapter VI of the UN Charter. The Canadian designation for its contribution to the UN Operation in Somalia (UNOSOM) was subsequently titled OP Cordon.

Under the UNOSOM structure, Somalia was to be split into five sectors. The Canadian contingent was slated to operate out of the Port of Bossasso and to share the area of the old British protectorate in northern and northeastern Somalia in coordination with an Australian battalion. Its tentative task was to provide security for the distribution of humanitarian relief, as well as to participate in limited local humanitarian projects. Not surprisingly, the choice of unit to fulfill Canada's latest UN obligation fell to the Canadian Airborne Regiment. It was no secret that the Airborne's "extended family" had lobbied hard to find a mission for the ebullient paratroopers, particularly in view of the recent string of events, and their pleas had not fallen on deaf ears.

The decision to send the Airborne Regiment, however, was not welcomed by all. The nature of the mission required the Airborne to be re-equipped with the Grizzly Armoured Vehicle General Purpose (AVGP). This could only be accomplished at the expense of existing mechanized units. In addition, the Regiment was also logically required to re-orientate from a parachute/light infantry role to a mechanized one. Given the very brief original three-week preparation period, the enormity of the task caused some anxiety. To further exacerbate the silent debate, a rash of disciplinary incidents, particularly in relation to 2 Commando, brought back to the fore difficulties which had not been adequately dealt with following the Hewson Report. Incidents including the destruction of personal property, the illegal use of pyrotechnics, the discharge of weapons in a provincial park, excessive alcohol consumption, and the burning of a duty-NCO's vehicle justifiably raised angst.

Further apprehension stemmed from the SSF Commander's concern that there was a definite lack of focus behind the unit's haphazard training approach. Brigadier-General Ernie Beno's critical assessment was confirmed during Exercise Stalwart Providence, the brigade-controlled evaluation of the Canadian Airborne Regiment's operational readiness. Serious shortcomings,

"Iron Canopies." 3 Mech Cdo on parade in Baden, Germany, 29 June 1973.   *(CAFM)*

specifically the absence of Regimental Standard Operating Procedures (SOPs) became evident. The SSF Commander was clearly not impressed. At the end of the exercise he refused to declare the unit "operationally ready." Instead he prescribed supplementary training, specifically to overcome the problems associated with the lack of regimental standardization. Additionally, the paratroopers were directed to complete more mission-specific activity in regard to humanitarian-type assignments.

More dramatic was the dismissal of the commanding officer of the Cdn AB Regt. This extreme step was primarily taken due to the CO's failure to adequately prepare the Regiment for deployment.

The drastic measures seemed to work. By mid November the paratroopers were declared "operationally ready." The improvements were such that the SSF Commander later declared that the Airborne Regiment represented the best unit Canada possessed to meet the exacting and warlike conditions of the looming Somalia mission.

The change in the unit's status, however, was soon moot. Delays in receiving an actual deployment date soon clouded the mood of the optimistic paratroopers. The mission which was to be launched by the end of September had now dragged well into November. Significantly, by month-end events quickly unravelled. The security council adopted a new option which fundamentally changed the entire scope of the mission. The new mandate, in accordance with Security Council Resolution 794, called for enforcement action under Chapter VII of the United Nation's Charter. Almost overnight, the mission evolved from peacekeeping to peace-making. Consequently, the paratroopers were no longer tasked with trying to maintain the peace, but rather were now responsible for imposing it on the antagonists, by the use of force if necessary. Accordingly, OP Cordon was suspended on 2 December, and two days later was formally cancelled. On 5 December a new Warning Order was issued. The national designation for Canada's participation in the new American-led enforcement operation entitled the Unified Task Force (UNITAF), was OP Deliverance. The paratroopers were now officially part of the newly crafted peace-making mandate.

The change in status was clearly enunciated. The Chief of Defence Staff, General Jean de Chastelain, announced that the new mission was a "peace enforcement action to ease the suffering of the Somalian people." "The contingent," he explained, "was authorized terms of engagement to take all steps to ensure that the job gets done."

Within the UNITAF mission, the paratroopers were specifically tasked with providing a secure environment for the distribution of humanitarian relief supplies in the Canadian Humanitarian Relief Sector (HRS), an area covering approximately thirty thousand square kilometres. This was translated into tasks which included: the security of airports; the protection of food convoys; the protection of food distribution centres; the rebuilding of infrastructure including roads, bridges and schools; the re-establishment of a local police force in Belet Huen and numerous other humanitarian projects.

However, the Cdn AB Regt experienced disciplinary problems in theatre which detracted from its actual performance. Incidents including: the mistreatment of prisoners on several occasions, the alleged unjustified shooting and resultant death of an intruder; and the torture death of an apprehended thief ultimately defined the Airborne's achievements in the public consciousness.

Unfortunately, selective cases of poor leadership and the criminal actions of a few in the dusty wasteland of Somalia laid the foundation for the Regiment's eventual demise. The sandstorm which swirled around the small number of appalling events which transpired, collectively covered the paratroopers with such notoriety that the Canadian Airborne Regiment Battle Group's (Cdn AB Regt BG) accomplishments were completely obliterated. Objectively examined, the Airborne's actual contribution to the amelioration of the suffering in Somalia was extremely laudable.

The paratroopers arrived in Somalia during the hottest time of the year, December 1992-January 1993, into conditions that were later acknowledged to be "as extreme as Canadian troops have ever encountered." Aside from the temperature, the soldiers were faced with the threat of diseases such as cholera, hepatitis, malaria, typhoid, tuberculosis and numerous others. Venomous insects and snakes were widespread and tenacious parasites were virtually unavoidable. In addition, all

Winter exercise in Grays Flat, Alberta, 1973.

(Don Halcrow)

106mm recoiless rifle ready for action. *(CAFM)*

Armoured lifeline. APCs of "D" Company conducted the evacuation of numerous UN personnel as well as individuals from foreign embassies, 16 August 1974.
(WO W.H. Cole, CFPU CNL, Neg. CYPC-74-99)

In the Combat Zone, Tpr Bob Jones and Cpl Maurice Paul McManus, ready the machine gun on their APC on 5 August 1974, at the "American Club," in Nicosia, Cyprus.
(Photographer unknown, CFPU CNL, Neg. CYPC-74-22)

local water, even when boiled, was undrinkable. To further complicate operations, the Canadian area of responsibility was home to the militia formations of the three most powerful faction leaders in Somalia. Furthermore, the Canadian zone also encompassed the turbulent Ethiopian border. In spite of these formidable obstacles, the Cdn AB Regt BG actively proceeded to fulfill its mandate. Their unremitting physical presence, achieved through a combination of dialogue and military operations, soon created an atmosphere of control, dominance, and security. The Airborne program was so successful that the Belet Huen HRS was declared secure by UNITAF Headquarters in a period of less than three months.

As remarkable as the Airborne Regiment Battle Group's pacification program was, its humanitarian effort was even more praiseworthy. Hugh Tremblay, the Director of Humanitarian Relief and Rehabilitation in Somalia, used the paratroopers as a model for others. "If you want to know and to see what you should do while you are here in Somalia," he repeatedly told visitors, "go to Belet Huen, talk to the Canadians and do what they have done, emulate the Canadians and you will have success in your humanitarian relief sector." Similarly, Robert Press, a writer for the Christian Science Monitor wrote, "Belet Huen appears to be a model in Somalia for restoring peace and effectively using foreign troops during this country's transition from anarchy to a national government." Accolades from UN mandarins and UNITAF military commanders were equally as profuse. Jonathan T. Howe, the Special Representative to the UN Secretary-General stated, "the outstanding work of your unit [Cdn AB Regt BG] in its area of operations in both military and humanitarian aspects of the mission has been outstanding." Robert Oakley, the American Special Envoy to Somalia, asserted, "there is no question but that their [Cdn AB Regt BG] discipline, operational readiness, immediate responsiveness to assigned tasks, care and use of equipment, and ability to operate effectively in difficult climatic conditions were considered to be at the very top of all UNITAF units." Lieutenant-General R.B. Johnston, the American UNITAF Commander himself, similarly commented, "The Canadian Airborne Regiment has performed with great distinction and the Canadian

people should view its role in this historic humanitarian mission with enormous pride."

Tribute from Canadian diplomats was initially equally as generous. Barbara McDougall, the Secretary of State for External Affairs, professed that Canadian paratroopers had performed a "modern miracle," and the Canadian High Commissioner to Somalia, Her Excellency Lucie Edwards, declared that the paratroopers "have only added lustre to their reputation as peacekeepers."

The flattering tribute was well deserved. In total the Canadian Airborne Regiment Battle Group's achievements included: the formation of five local committees to restore local government; the conduct of approximately sixty humanitarian convoys which provided aid to ninety-six villages; the construction of four schools attended by 5,400 students at the end of the tour; the instruction and training of 272 school teachers; the supervision and training of local doctors and nurses; the training of 150 policemen in Belet Huen, 20 in Matabaan and 15 in St. Emily; the provision of potable water to local refugees; the repair of approximately twenty wells; the repair of village generators; the repair of the Belet Huen and Matabaan hospitals; the construction of a bridge; and the repair of over 200 kilometres of road. Tragically, despite their commendable achievements, the mission was redefined in the media and the public consciousness as a failure.

As a result of the poor leadership and criminal acts of a few, the paratroopers collectively became outcasts. The inexplicable and lamentable torture killing of Shidane Arone became the defining image of the Airborne's operation in Africa. Incredibly, the tenacious focus on the scandal which followed buried the reality of the Canadian Airborne Regiment Battle Group's true accomplishments.

This redefinition of the Somalia mission impacted dramatically on the Cdn AB Regt. The overwhelmingly negative media pushed condemnation of the paratroopers to new heights. Depicted as killers and racists in the press, neither the paratroopers nor their families, could expect an outpouring of overt support. Any attempted defence of the Regiment was quickly assailed by the media. Predictably, the paratroopers were placed under unprecedented examination by both military and public institutions. This continuing scrutiny eventually prompted the CDS to formally establish *The Board of Inquiry (BOI)-Canadian Airborne Regiment Battle Group* (known informally as the de Faye Commission), on 28 April 1993. The BOI was given the mandate to "investigate the leadership, discipline, operations, actions and procedures of the Airborne Battle Group." The board's existence, however, was measured in mere months as it was suspended pending the completion of a number of judicial proceedings. The BOI never resumed its work and was later eclipsed by the *Commission of Inquiry into the Deployment of Canadian Forces to Somalia* (commonly referred to as the Somalia Commission). Nonetheless, the Board did publish its Phase I Report in late-summer 1993. The CDS, Admiral John Anderson, was pleased with the results. He wrote, "I am heartened by the overriding conclusions of the report which state that the 'efforts and accomplishments of the Canadian Forces personnel in Somalia, in general, and the Canadian Airborne Regiment in particular, were truly outstanding and that there has been no evidence presented to the Board which would indicate any systemic problem within the Canadian Airborne Regiment which should, in any way, limit its usefulness or employability.'"

However, the BOI, unlike the Hewson Report, did not appease the critics. Even an internal DND review insisted that certain conclusions did not appear to be borne out by the actual testimony heard. It suggested that there had been enough evidence before the de Faye Commission to suggest that leadership problems reached up the chain of command to Canadian Joint Forces Somalia Headquarters (CJFS HQ) and that there were documents which indicated direct attempts to cover up facts behind several of the high-profile incidents which transpired in Somalia. The chairman of the internal review, Major-General Jean Boyle, further concluded that the most pressing issue regarding the Canadian Airborne Regiment was leadership. The BOI and its aftermath — the commencement of a series of courts-martial for those charged with wrong-doing or misconduct during OP Deliverance — and the ongoing media scrutiny all ensured that the spotlight remained focussed on the ostracized paratroopers.

Nevertheless, the Cdn AB Regt attempted to rebuild its shattered image in the wake of the continuing controversy. The first overt manifestation of the efforts at rebuilding came on 15 September 1993, with the dismissal of the Canadian Airborne Regiment's Commanding Officer, Lieutenant-Colonel D.C.A. Mathieu. The reassignment was delicately defined by the Army Commander as "an administrative procedure designed to ensure the transparency of the legal and disciplinary process." Regardless of how it was packaged, it allowed for the appointment of an officer who held a strong reputation as an exceptional field soldier and strict no-nonsense disciplinarian. There was no doubt within the ranks of the paratroopers that Lieutenant-Colonel Peter Kenward was sent to "clean house." Kenward represented the "line in the sand." If the Airborne Regiment was to re-establish its reputation, words would no longer be enough. Redemption was only possible by visibly demonstrating that the unit was the most operationally ready battalion in the Canadian Forces.

The rebuilding process was also the motive behind the transfer of the NATO ACE Mobile Force (Land) (AMF(L)) role to the paratroopers. This was perceived by Airborne supporters as a means of solidifying the Regiment's place in the Army organization, as well as of providing a rationale for restructuring the Regiment with a view to increasing its manpower and equipment. Not surprisingly, an internal reorganization designed to improve the Regiment's organic combat capability in consonance with its new task, was soon undertaken. By the end of September 1993, the Airborne's strength had increased from 601 to 665 all ranks. The expansion was due to the addition of an Air Defence Platoon and an Airborne Engineer Platoon within the Combat Support Commando. In tandem with the restructuring was the introduction of a specific mandate intended to provide a clear aim for the airborne soldiers to focus on.

The imposing, but unofficial, mission statement defined the requirement as, "the parachute delivery of 540 personnel, 12 vehicles and over 50 tons of combat supplies, at night, from 650 feet 'Above Ground Level' (AGL), onto one or more Drop Zones, with the complete force on the ground in less than 10 minutes."

Armoured lifeline. Paratroopers in APCs rescue US personnel on 19 August 1974, after an anti-American demonstration at the US Embassy. The American ambassador and several other individuals were killed.

(WO W.H. Cole, CFPU CNL, Neg. CYPC-74-156)

This Lynx armoured reconnaissance vehicle ran afoul of an anti-tank mine near the Blue Beret Camp near Nicosia, Cyprus, 15 August 1974. The crew escaped with no injuries. *(WO W.H. Cole, CFPU CNL, Neg. CYPC-74-96)*

James Richardson, the Minister of Defence, speaks to a group of sceptical paratroopers, Ledra Palace, Nicosia, Cyprus, 1974.
(Don Halcrow)

A 500 lb Turkish bomb lands in the Plain of Lizards near the Blue Beret Camp, 1974.   *(Don Halcrow)*

To the rescue of comrades. Paratroopers in APCs rush to evacuate Swedish peacekeepers who came under fire.   *(Don Halcrow)*

Regimental exercise off the West Coast, near Tofino, BC.

(Don Halcrow and CAFM)

The realm of the operational was not the only area of focus. The Cdn AB Regt worked diligently at redeeming its tattered image in all spheres. In addition to a challenging and gruelling training schedule, the Canadian Airborne Regiment demonstrated its prowess in the competitive arena. The paratroopers won the 1994 Canadian Forces Small Arms Competition. This included the esteemed Queen's Medal for the top-scoring individual marksman in the CF. The Airborne also won the vaunted Hamilton Gault Trophy awarded to the infantry battalion with the highest unit aggregate score for its annual marksmanship results, as well as timings for the two (Army) mandatory ten-mile "forced marches" conducted on two consecutive days. Furthermore, the Regimental team, representing Canada, won the prestigious North European Command Infantry Competition (NECIC) with the most commanding Canadian performance in the competition's history.

The amelioration of the Regiment's fortunes was deceiving. In the summer of 1994, the Regiment was tasked to support two separate missions deploying to Rwanda, Africa. A pair of platoons were dispatched to provide the security element for both OP Passage, a Canadian-sponsored humanitarian mission, and OP Lance, the Canadian designation for its participation in the UN Assistance Mission for Rwanda (UNAMIR). The paratroopers once again demonstrated their worth. Reports of mass killings in the southeast region of Rwanda necessitated the rapid dispatch of the Airborne platoon attached to 1 Canadian Division Signals and Headquarters Regiment to that area of the country. Their task was to provide a presence to increase the confidence of the population and to determine the verity of the rumours. Their resultant performance earned them the unbridled praise of the UNAMIR II Commander. He wrote the Canadian Chief of Defence Staff stating, "the local government and military commanders were convinced that the Canadians had deployed at least one and perhaps two companies into the sector. Most of the villages in the sector were deserted at the beginning. After constant patrolling of all villages, the people gained confidence in the level of security afforded them and started to return." Three weeks after the mission's commencement, the exhausted paratroopers, numbering less than forty, passed responsibility for the sector to an entire Nigerian Infantry Battalion which arrived to replace them.

Unfortunately, despite the Regiment's notable achievements since its return from Somalia, there was just no escaping the incidents which had transpired in the Horn of Africa. Events after the actual killings transformed the issue from one of a series of criminal acts, compounded by poor leadership, to one of national scandal. The brutality of a number of paratroopers became eclipsed by the spectre of an alleged cover-up. The well-known Canadian editorialist, Peter Worthington observed that the "Somalia incidents that provoked the inquiry have almost become irrelevant." The continuing drama ensured that an unrelenting scrutiny was maintained on the Cdn AB Regt. The most minor foible committed by a paratrooper became national news.

Nonetheless, 1995 ushered in a new year of hope for the airborne unit. On 5 January 1995, it was announced that the Canadian Airborne Regiment had been chosen to replace 1 RCR in Sector South, in Croatia, in the coming spring. The airborne soldiers were being given an opportunity to prove themselves on another operational tour.

Regrettably, whether this attempt at salvation would have extinguished the Airborne's notoriety became a moot point. On 15 January 1995, the CTV television network broadcast excerpts from a video made by soldiers of 2 Commando during their tour in Somalia. The video clips depicted several paratroopers making racial slurs and behaving in an unprofessional manner.

The tempest had broken once again. Media reaction was trenchant, as was the resultant political reaction. The apparition of Somalia once again emerged to haunt the Regiment. The stage was now set for the mortal blow, delivered a mere three days later. Another amateur video, this time portraying a 1992, 1Commando "initiation party," utterly devastated what was left of the Canadian Airborne Regiment's image.

The tape showed 1 Commando soldiers involved in activities which were degrading, disgusting, and with racist overtones. Its release not only embarrassed the government and the Canadian Forces but shocked the sensibilities of the general public. It quickly became apparent that the unacceptable spectacle, although dated, alienated any remaining support. It also cleared the way for the destruction of the Cdn AB Regt.

The minister of national defence swiftly ordered an investigation. Ominously, shortly after the airing of the video Prime Minister Jean Chrétien bluntly conceded, "if we have to dismantle it [Canadian Airborne Regiment], we'll dismantle it. I have no problem with that at all."

The Army's report on the incident was submitted to the minister of national defence on 23 January. It stated that an objective analysis of the facts demonstrated that the current Airborne Regiment was distinctly different from the unit in Somalia. It concluded that a "line in the sand" had truly been drawn.

However, during the course of the investigation, the disclosure of a third video depicting yet another 1 Commando initiation ceremony, this time from the summer of 1994, undermined this argument. Although the behaviour depicted in the most recent tape was not as offensive as that of the preceding video, the fact that this type of forbidden activity had still been occurring so recently merely confirmed latent suspicions.

An official press release was scheduled for the same afternoon that the final report was presented. At this time, David Collenette, the Minister of National Defence announced, "although our senior military officers believe the Regiment as constituted should continue, the government believes it cannot. Therefore, today under the authority of the National Defence Act, I have ordered the disbandment of the Canadian Airborne Regiment." The defence minister explained that the conduct of some members of the Airborne Regiment over the past few years had denigrated the reputation of all members, past and present, and brought into question the trust others bestowed on the Canadian Forces. The "cumulative effect on the public's confidence in the Regiment," concluded Collenette, "led me to conclude that the Regiment had to be disbanded."

As a result, on 4 and 5 March 1995, the elaborate and well-attended final disbandment ceremonies were conducted in CFB Petawawa. The emotionally charged weekend bore testimony to a large number of paratroopers, who had always prided themselves on their ability to withstand hardship and pain without so much as a murmur, sobbing shamelessly into the arms of their loved ones. In spite of the circumstances, or more accurately because of them, Lieutenant-Colonel Kenward delivered an address capturing the essence of the airborne spirit permeating the ceremonies. He asserted, "Let the message be clear. Those of us who serve the Regiment today are not moving on in disgrace. We have loyally and very credibly carried the standard of soldiering excellence passed to us from those paratroopers who came before. We need not look down but continue to hold our heads high and stare straight ahead, knowing we stood in the door and were always ready to do our duty."

The cycle had come full circle. On 6 May 1968, during Colonel D.H. Rochester's opening address to the Regiment, he had declared, "ahead lies the great adventure of this new regiment." And so it came to pass — the end of an era, the end of the great adventure. In what can be construed as a final irony, the notorious and widely perceived villainous Canadian Airborne Regiment passed obediently and quietly into the annals of Canadian military history.

Clockwise from above: Heavy equipment drop during a winter exercise in Wainwright, Alberta, 1974. *(Don Halcrow)*; Spartan facilities — an Airborne HQ. *(CAFM)*; Internal Security training for OP Gamescan (1976 Olympics). *(CAFM)*; Paratroopers rehearse helicopter drills during OP Gamescan during the 1976 Montreal Olympics. The Canadian Airborne Regiment was tasked as a Rapid Reaction Force as part of the Canadian Forces security responsibilities. *(Johnson, CFPU CNL, Neg. IMOC 76-818)*; First light exercise drop onto Gray Flats, Alberta. *(Don Halcrow)*

1 Cdo paratroopers deploy into Camp Wainwright, Alberta, during Ex Rapier Thrust V, 16 January 1977.   (R22R Archives)

Full equipment ramp jump from a C-130 Hercules into Fort MacMurray, over the tar sands, Alberta, 1976.   (Don Halcrow)

The Regiment conducted its final mass drop on DZ Buxton in Edmonton on 3 July 1977, prior to its controversial move to CFB Petawawa.
(CAFM)

Continuation drops onto DZ Buxton.   *(Don Halcrow)*

Continuation drops onto DZ Buxton. *(Don Halcrow)*

Mass Drop. *(Photographer unknown, CFPU CNL, Neg. PCN 75-936)*

Mock Tower, CABC, CFB Edmonton, October 1980.   *(Photographer unknown, CFPU CNL, Neg. IOC 81-2006)*

J. Dextraze, the CDS, escorted by the Special Service Force Commander, Brigadier-General Andrew Christie, inspects members of the Cdn AB Regt on the occasion of the first official parade marking the inclusion of the Regiment into the SSF.   *(Cpl Bailey, CFPU CNL, Neg. IS-77-344)*

Left and right: Members of "E" Airborne Battery, 2 RCHA, scramble to recover an L-5 Howitzer and ready it for firing during Ex Mobile Warrior, 3 October 1977.
(Lt G. Wragg, CFPU CNL, Neg. ISC-77-1132)   *(Lt G. Wragg, CFPU CNL, Neg. ISC-77-1127)*

Left and right: Live fire exercise in Camp Meaford, Ontario, 1979.   *(Don Halcrow.)*

DZ Anzio, CFB Petawawa, completed in 1980.   *(CAFM)*   The dreaded Mock Tower in CFB Petawawa.   *(CAFM)*

143

Defence of Canada Operations. Paratroopers participate in Ex Optic Nerve, January 1981. *(CAFM)*

Defence of Canada Operations, Ex Optic Nerve, January 1981. *(CAFM)*

Top left: Ex Border Star, Fort Bliss, Texas, 1985. *(CAFM)*; Clockwise from top right: three photographs of Desert Survival training, Fort Bliss, Texas, 1985.

(CAFM)

Top left: Lethal payload from a stormy sky. *(CAFM)*; Enemy Force. The American opposing force search for the elusive paratroopers during Ex Border Star, Fort Bliss Texas, 1985.

(CAFM)

Jumpmaster's check during Ex Border Star, El Paso, Texas, March 1985.   *(Brakele, CFPU CNL, Neg. IOC 85-197)*

Blind faith in one's comrades. The Jumpmaster's check. *(CAFM)*

Regimental Colour Party marching through the streets of El Paso, Texas, as a finale to Exercise Border Star, 1985. *(CAFM)*

The winning 3 Cdo team of the 2 RCHA Obstacle Course Race in Cyprus, 1986.
(Dave Lavery)

HRH Prince Charles chats with Regimental officers in Cyprus, 1986, as part of the ceremonies which formally affiliated the Canadian Airborne Regiment with the British Parachute Regiment. *(CAFM)*

"GO!" *(CAFM)*

Ramp exit water drop into Lake Ontario, Kingston. *(Don Halcrow)*

"GO!" *(CAFM)*

Parachute drop onto DZ Anzio, CFB Petawawa. *(Don Halcrow)*

Water drop into Lake Ontario. The empty canopy is the result of one paratrooper cutting away his canopy too early (at 180 feet). The individual survived but was knocked unconscious on impact and suffered bruised kidneys and a dislocated hip. *(Don Halcrow)*

MCpl Emanuel Pacheco crosses the finish line to win the 1986 SSF Ironman Competition. The race consisted of a 46 kilometre course, broken down into a 25 km rucksack run, a 200 metre water obstacle crossing with a canoe, a 4.8 km portage, 12 km of canoeing and a final 4 km sprint over the sandy Mattawa Plain, CFB Petawawa. The winning time was 5 hours and 48 minutes. *(CAFM)*

Cramped confines. The bowels of the C-130 Hercules provides little space for comfort. During long deployments the paratroopers would conduct "in-flight" dressing. *(CAFM)*

Soldiers from "E" Bty, 2 RCHA, prepare to embark a C-130 Hercules aircraft as part of a Tactical Airlift Exercise (TALEX 8806), 21 January 1989.

(Sgt Reid, CFPU CNL, Neg. IOC 89-2-7)

The defence of the North, specifically the ability to rapidly deploy paratroopers to any corner of the nation's territory, represented the Regiment's most pervasive as well as persistent task.

(Canadian Parachute Centre, CPC)

Winter continuation drop, CFB Petawawa. *(Don Halcrow)*

Clockwise from top left: The soldier's load. Paratroopers pulling a section toboggan while loaded down with their own personal rucksacks during winter warfare training in CFB Petawawa. *(CAFM)*; Airborne Headquarters, Exercise Lightning Strike, Goose Bay, Labrador, January 1986. *(CAFM)*; Winter exercise-Defence of Canada Operations, 1988. *(CAFM)*; Airborne Command Post, 1989. Conspicuously absent are the luxuries of shelter or vehicles. *(CAFM)*

En route for a winter MFP drop onto DZ Anzio, CFB Petawawa, 1988.

(*Don Halcrow*)

Clockwise from top left: MFP exit from a C-130 aircraft over CFB Petawawa, 1988. *(Don Halcrow)*; Military freefall parachuting is the entry method of choice for the Regiment's Pathfinder Platoon. *(CPC)*; An Iltis jeep is lowered unto the rigging platform in preparation for a drop. *(CAFM)*; The Canadian Airborne Regiment Colours on parade. *(CAFM)*

Top and bottom: Airborne Iltis TOW Anti-Tank system takes aim, 1989.

Clockwise from top left: Mountain School, Mount Yamaniska, Alberta, 1990. *(Eamonn Barry)*; Paratroopers hone their skills at mountain operations, CFB Petawawa. *(CAFM)*; Rappel into action from a CH-147 Huey Helicopter. *(CAFM)*; Mountain Operations training in the Canadian Rockies. *(CAFM)*

Airborne exercise with American Special Forces. *(CAFM)*

Top left: An exhausted paratrooper grabs some elusive sleep during the Reconnaissance Patrolman's course in the autumn of 1990. (*CAFM*); Top right: "Hoochie Hotel." (*CAFM*); Bottom left and right: Paratroopers clearing the inner bowels of the Arnprior Power Generating Station, during Exercise Power Raider, 1989. (*CAFM*)

Paratroopers undergoing a platoon assault under NBCW conditions, CFB Petawawa, 1987.   (*Don Halcrow*)

Masters of all environments, these paratroopers are conducting the final phase of the 1990 Regimental Mountain School. *(CAFM)*

Basic Recce Patrolman Course, CFB Petawawa, 1991. *(Eamonn Barry)*

Top and above: Paratroopers from 1 Cdo participating in a Jungle Warfare and Survival Course conducted by the French Foreign Legion, in Camp Zut, French Guyana, March 1991. *(Michel Purnelle)*

Opposite page: Royal Westminster Regiment refresher jump onto DZ Rochester, Chilliwack, BC.
(Capt Chuck MacKinnon)

Mass Drop. (CPC)

Left and right: The venerable C6 7.62mm GPMG supports the paratroopers' final assault. (CAFM)

Top and above: Paratroopers participate in the live-fire counter-ambush drills in preparation for OP Cordon, fall 1992. *(CAFM)*

Clockwise from top left: Sgt Eamonn Barry at the Belet Huen airport, January 1993. *(Eamonn Barry)*; Cpl Robert Prouse at his position on the perimeter of the airfield at Belet Huen, January 1993. *(Robert Prouse)*; Living quarters, Belet Huen airfield, January 1993. *(Robert Prouse)*; Living quarters, Belet Huen airfield, January 1993. *(Eamonn Barry)*

Belet Huen airfield, January 1993.   *(Eamonn Barry)*

Top: A 427 Sqn air reconnaissance patrol flies by the 2 Cdo compound in Somalia. *(CAFM)*; bottom: 1 Cdo compound, Somalia, January 1993. *(Michel Purnelle)*

Corporal Michel Purnelle surveys the ground beyond the 1 Cdo compound, February 1993. *(Michel Purnelle)*

A Shebelle River foot patrol searching for prohibited weapon caches. Pictured are Cpls Trevor Boudereau, Frank Mellish, and Ronson Okerlund. *(Ronson Okerlund)*

Eating dirt. A 3 Cdo vehicle patrol in the hinterland of the Belet Huen Humanitarian Sector.

(Ronson Okerlund)

Members of 8 Pl, 3 Cdo "cam-up" their "Grizzly" AVGP prior to commencing patrols in the Somalia hinterlands.

(Eamonn Barry)

Returning 1 Cdo mounted patrol, January 1993. *(Michel Purnelle)*

7 Pl, 3 Cdo, on patrol in the highlands east of the Mogadishu Highway, south of Belet Huen, 25 January 1993. *(Robert Prouse)*

Necessity is the mother of all invention. Expedient "vehicle jacks" were crafted by driving an AVGP onto a termite hill and digging out a groove under the tire.

(Photographer unknown, CFPU CNL, Neg. ISC 93-10371)

Tprs Bechard and Adam Thibault of 7 Pl, 3 Cdo, on patrol near Dhoqor, southeast of Belet Huen, January 1993. *(Robert Prouse)*

MCpl Pat Goodbody of 7 Pl, 3 Cdo, on patrol near Dhoqor, southeast of Belet Huen, January 1993. *(Robert Prouse)*

A 3 Cdo patrol near the Ethiopian border comes upon armour remnants of the Somali Army. *(Robert Prouse)*

Vehicle search in Zone 3. This effort resulted in the confiscation of one pistol, two AK-47s and several hundred kilos of drugs. *(CAFM)*

Corporal Turcotte attempts to calm members of the local population during a demonstration at the Belet Huen airfield, January 1993. *(CAFM)*

Above: Cpl Dave Whynot patrolling the village of Treejante, February 1993. (*Robert Prouse*); left: top; Cpl Mellish on foot patrol in Belet Huen. (*CAFM*); bottom; WO Wayne Bartlett conducting a vehicle check-point on the "Mogadishu Highway" in Somalia. (*Eamonn Barry*)

Paratroopers on a mounted patrol through Belet Huen.   *(CAFM)*

Sgt Eamonn Barry after the 28 March 1993 firefight. *(Eamonn Barry)*

Top and bottom right: Paratroopers conduct a search for weapons in an outlying village. *(CAFM)*

(Photographer unknown, CFPU CNL, Neg. ISC 93-10367)

Cpl Mellish delivers food to an ICRC feeding station in Belet Huen. *(CAFM)*

Canadian paratroopers descend to the desert floor as part of the Regimental birthday jump in Somalia. *(Ronson Okerlund)*

MCpl Gates Marino exits the CH-135 Twin Huey over DZ Pegasus, Somalia.
(Sgt Ed Dixon, CFPU CNL, Neg. ISC 93-10449)

MCpl Leclerc of 1 Cdo conducts a resupply of the most valuable commodity in Somalia, water. *(CAFM)*

Ever vigilant, Somalia 1993.

(CAFM)

Return from a 2 Cdo foot patrol in Belet Huen, Somalia 1993. The reality of an operational theatre — weapons first. *(CAFM)*

Casualty evacuation drills conducted during the Regimental Mountain School, CFB Petawawa, fall 1994. *(Robert Prouse)*

Ice climbing in Orient Bay, Ontario.
(Robert Prouse)

Final parachute drop of "E" Bty, 2 RCHA, onto DZ Anzio, CFB Petawawa. *(Cpl Clarke, CFPU CNL, Neg. PAC 93-366-[20])*

First jump with the Regiment. The ritualistic "camming" of the virgin jumper. *(CAFM)*

MCpl Innes and Cpl Gray in the process of dressing for a short tactical exercise. Their loads are actually light. They carry no ammunition, stores or rations required for an extended operation. Yet, they will carry far in excess of the loads of the normal infantryman. *(CAFM)*

The thrill is gone — leaving the DZ. *(CAFM)*

"Stand-By!"
(CAFM)

Clockwise from top left: Emplaning for a parachute insertion, Brown's Airfield, Petawawa. (*Robert Prouse*); Emplaning for an airborne exercise. (*Robert Prouse*); Final parachute drop of "E" Bty, 2 RCHA, onto DZ Anzio, CFB Petawawa. Note the "A" at the bottom left which marks the leading edge of the DZ (release point). (*Cpl Clarke, CFPU CNL, Neg. PAC 93-366-[1-21], wallet 8919.*); Paratroopers conduct a ramp jump from a C-130 Hercules over DZ Anzio, in CFB Petawawa, 11 August 1994. (*Robert Prouse, CFPU CNL, Neg. PAC 94-468-[1-21]*)

Prince Andrew, inspects the Regiment during the 25th Anniversary
Celebrations, September 1993. *(Robert Prouse)*

The Colonel-in-Chief of the Cdn AB Regt, His Royal Highness Prince Andrew, addresses paratroopers prior to a jump, September 1993.   *(CAFM)*

Orders for Ex Pegasus Blizzard, January 1994.   *(Robert Prouse)*

Top: left; En-route to the RV after another successful drop, Ex Pegasus Blizzard, January 1994. *(Robert Prouse)*; right; Actions after landing, DZ Anzio, CFB Petawawa, 1994. *(Eamonn Barry)*; bottom left and right: Landing sequence of a heavily burdened paratrooper during Exercise Pegasus Blizzard, January 1994, in CFB Petawawa. *(CAFM)*

Cpl Tremblay, of Direct Fire Support Platoon, patiently waits with his .50 cal MG for the enemy, Ex Pegasus Blizzard, January 1994. *(Robert Prouse)*

Moving into the assault position, Ex Pegasus Blizzard, January 1994. *(Robert Prouse)*

On the ragged outer edge. A recurring theme — the paratrooper on the edge of civilization, reliant only on himself and his comrades. A paratrooper from 3 Cdo surveys the barren mountainous landscape in Northern Norway during an AMF(L) exercise. *(Bernd Horn)*

Lethal predators. Airborne snipers, Sgt Frank Moses and Trevor Downing, patiently survey their surroundings during Ex Falcon Prey, 7-9 March 1994. *(Bernd Horn)*

Cpl Craig Turcotte demonstrating his latent talent at building igloos in Gjoa Haven, NWT, March 1994. *(Bernd Horn)*

Top and bottom: Regimental drop during Ex Pegasus Fighter, onto DZ Fryar in Fort Benning, Georgia, May 1994. *(Bernd Horn)*

Paratroopers practising improvised obstacle crossings in Fort Benning, May 1994. *(Bernd Horn)*

Airborne snipers in customized "Gillie"suits. *(Bernd Horn)*

Top and bottom: 3 Cdo prepares to assault a fortified compound at K22 Range in Fort Benning. *(CAFM)*

Paratroopers conducting live fire house-clearing drills in Fort Benning.   (CAFM)

Ex Normandy Salute — the 50th Anniversary of the mass drop into Ranville, France, 5 June 1994. *(CAFM)*

LCol Peter Kenward awards a group of US Rangers their Canadian Jump
Wings.   *(Robert Prouse)*

Members of 3 Cdo march off parade during D-Day 50th Anniversary ceremonies in Gosport, UK, 4 June 1994. *(CAFM)*

The 1994 CFSAC Champions. Cpl Carlos Arevelo (seated) was the year's Queen Medalist (top shot in the CF). *(Robert Prouse)*

First-in! Airborne Pathfinders conducting an MFP insertion. *(Robert Prouse)*

Cpl Dunn checking the outer perimeter wire of the 1 CDHSR base camp at Amahoro Stadium, Kigali, Rwanda. *(Photographer unknown, CFPU CNL, Neg. ISC 94-2001)*

Cpls Okerlund, Brown and Gudnason pose with a Bangladeshi vehicle that was hastily abandoned in the expeditious flight from Kigali during the conflict. *(Ronson Okerlund)*

Maj Bernd Horn and Capt Dave Simpkin pose with a fourteen-year-old, three-year veteran of the Rwandan People's Army (RPA), now a bodyguard for a senior official of the new RPA government. *(Bernd Horn)*

Cpl Dave Dunn poses with a child soldier from the Rwandan People's Army. *(Ronson Okerlund)*

Typical RPA mobile patrol. *(Ronson Okerlund)*

Cpls Howlett and Callis construct a bunker on the outside of Amahoro Stadium in Kigali, Rwanda. *(CAFM)*

WO Wayne Bartlett, the 8 Platoon Second in Command, conducts a briefing at the Pegasus Primus patrol base. *(Ronson Okerlund)*

The Pegasus Primus patrol base was located in an abandoned brewery. This base was used for maintenance and resupply of the mobile patrols which scoured Sector 2B. Vehicle patrols normally conducted 24-48 hour missions. *(Ronson Okerlund)*

The difficult terrain in areas of Sector 2B necessitated a dismounted paratrooper to prove the route for the platoon vehicles. *(Ronson Okerlund)*

Eight Platoon passes through a typical main street of an above-average-sized town in Sector 2B, Rwanda. *(Ronson Okerlund)*

Dismounted patrol two kilometres from the Rwandan/Tanzanian border.
(Ronson Okerlund)

Natural beauty and rolling terrain of Sector 2B.

(Ronson Okerlund)

Back in Africa. Cpls Johnny Evans, Dave Dunn, Wayne Howlett and Ronson Okerlund take a break in the lush jungle of the highlands in Rwandan. Contrary to their experience in Somalia, the threat environment in Rwanda was low and the population friendly.

(Ronson Okerlund)

An 8 Platoon patrol halts to investigate allegations of mass killings in Sector 2B. *(Ronson Okerlund)*

Top and bottom: An absence of humanity. Paratroopers discover a churchyard in Sector 2B littered with the victims of genocide.
(Ronson Okerlund)

Eight Pl, 3 Cdo, assigned as the D & S Platoon for 1 CDSHR as part of OP Lance, conducts a patrol stop in Sector 2B, Rwanda. The vehicles adopted a triangular patrol base formation for security.   (*Ronson Okerlund*)

Weapons maintenance during a patrol stop in an abandoned village in Sector 2B.   (*Ronson Okerlund*)

Top and above: Paratroopers jumping from a Canadian C-130 Hercules and an American C-117 Starlifter aircraft as part of the Regimental Mass Drop, 4 March 1995. *(Robert Prouse)*

The Cdn AB Regt, on parade during the SSF Farewell to the Canadian Airborne Regiment ceremony, 1 March 1995.

(Robert Prouse)

The Regiment with its Colours marches off DZ Anzio after the Farewell Mass Drop, 4 March 1995. *(Don Halcrow)*

The final inspection of the Regiment, 4 March 1995. (*Robert Prouse*)

The final march-past. L - R: Cpls Evans, Watson, CSM Vienneau, Cpl Ferguson. (*CAFM*)

The CO, LCol Peter Kenward, signs the disbandment document, Nicklin Parade Square, CFB Petawawa, 4 March 1995. *(Robert Prouse)*

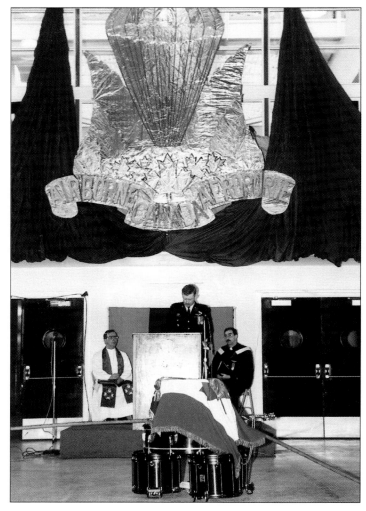

Laying-up the Colours, RCR Drill Hall, Y101, CFB Petawawa,
5 March 1995.   *(Brian Rye)*

The Cdn AB Regt marching past the "Into Action" Statue located at the gate of CFB Petawawa, 5 March 1995, as part of the laying-up of the Colours ceremony.

(*Robert Prouse*)

Cdn AB Regt commemorative plaque, Nicklin Parade Square, CFB Petawawa. *(Bernd Horn)*

PART V

IN THE AFTERMATH OF DISBANDMENT

SURVIVAL OF A CAPABILITY

1995-1999

he disbandment of the Canadian Airborne Regiment reignited a perennial and often malevolent debate. Did Canada require an airborne capability? If so, how large and for what specific purpose? Since 1940, the argument had been repeatedly revisited and studied in great depth.

Unquestionably, airborne soldiering, true to General Allard's original intent, provided a forum for challenging and dynamic training not available elsewhere. More importantly, it developed unrivalled individual and light infantry skills. The experience gathered in the Regiment served a critical "cross-pollination" function. The individual fieldcraft, leadership, navigation, and patrolling skills, developed and honed in the Airborne, provided the mechanized infantry battalions with a vital infusion of much-needed expertise. It was a generally accepted maxim that "airborne service just makes a good soldier that much better."

Brigadier-General Bruce Jeffries, the SSF Commander at the time of disbandment, highlighted the contribution of the airborne soldiers to the Army. He professed, "the Regiment has defined the concept of teamwork and has given each of us a better understanding of our potential.

Cpls Chalmers and Callis leading the way. (Robert Prouse)

Since arriving in Petawawa in 1977, it [Cdn AB Regt] has set the pace and the Brigade and Base have had to change gears to keep up. This example will be sorely missed."

The demise of the Canadian Airborne Regiment also represented the forfeiture of the capability to rapidly project national power, whether for domestic or international crises. However, it is not necessarily clear whether this is essential, much less desirable in the present environment. Factors such as the likely risk or threat to security, alternate forces available, and the prevailing fiscal climate, must all be taken into account. With the de facto removal of the Regiment from the Army "Order of Battle," the opportunity to redefine the structure of Canada's airborne capability became possible. The circumstances which brought this reality about foreshadowed its less-than-prominent future.

As tenuous as the continued existence of airborne forces appeared, the nation's enormous geographical endowment seemingly ensured that a niche for paratroopers remained. However, in the immediate aftermath of the disbandment announcement, no plan was announced for the fulfilment of the airborne role, in either the short or long term. It was only during the ensuing turmoil and confusion of closing down the Regiment, literally a scant few days prior to the officially directed 5 March date, that a missive was received from Army headquarters which addressed the potential dilemma. The belated message declared that "there are some outstanding operational tasks for which [sic] an element of the Regiment must be prepared to execute." Therefore, the Army commander directed the commanding officer of the Canadian Airborne Holding Unit, the designation given to the remaining elements of the Canadian Airborne Regiment as of 6 March, to develop a company-sized group (based primarily on RCR members), not in excess of three hundred personnel, with appropriate command and control, as well as elements of Airborne Service Commando, to provide contingency troops in the event of short-notice operations. Ten days later a more detailed message underlining the necessity of an airborne capability, was dispatched by Army headquarters. The latest directive emphasized the fact that "Canadians will not accept the contention that we cannot put troops on the ground anywhere in this country at anytime." As a result, the fate of the Canadian paratrooper, in some form or another, was assured.

A second "airborne bridge," analogous to that created by the Canadian SAS Company of the post-Second World War era, was formed. 3 Commando, now redesignated 3 Commando Group, was brought back to life with an increased authorized strength of 187 paratroopers. Individual and sub-unit equipment which had been cleaned and packed away was now reissued. In addition, a training plan was quickly resurrected.

The establishment of 3 Commando Group, which now represented Canada's interim airborne capability, officially took effect 6 March 1995. In the span of a few short days Canada's provisional parachute force went from the brink of oblivion to a state of continual high readiness. The 3 Commando Group was on a perpetual footing that required it to be capable of deploying on operations within forty-eight hours of notification. It was specifically tasked as a vanguard to: "conduct territorial and continental defence operations; conduct domestic/ regional tasks; conduct surveillance and reconnaissance of the Canadian land mass to demonstrate national presence; and as an Immediate Reaction Force Vanguard for domestic operations for employment in areas where conventional forces could not be deployed in a timely fashion."

Training, which had ceased with the defence minister's announcement in January, now quickly returned to its former hectic pace. The focus of parachuting also returned to a strictly tactical orientation. The 3 Commando Group activities included demonstrations on airmobile planning and execution, as well as the conduct of a comprehensive live-fire battle school. In addition, a busy cycle of urban warfare, internal security and demolition training was capped by a demonstration on the importance and viability of airborne troops. The presentation took the form of a three-aircraft Commando Group operation designated Exercise Lethal Reach, specifically designed to display the flexibility, speed and strategic capability of airborne forces. The paratroopers jumped into DZ Lindsay Valley, in CFB Gagetown, New Brunswick, on the night of 6 June to strike a hypothetical insurgent staging base. Despite a poor drop, the target was successfully neutralized, and the paratroopers were back at their home base in Petawawa, Ontario, in less than thirty-six hours. The greatest delay was waiting for aircraft. 3 Commando Group confirmed a central tenet of airborne forces, namely the ability to reach out and influence a situation half a country away, literally in hours.

The fate of the nation's paratroopers, however, was anything but nirvana. The recently released 1994 White Paper made absolutely no mention of airborne or parachute forces. The Army commander asserted that there was an implicit parachute requirement, "primarily in a domestic context," lodged in the provision of multi-purpose, combat-capable land forces. The struggle to define how this "implied" capability would be structured was tacit. Recent history and a long collective memory ensured that the airborne lobby within the Army was impotent in its ability to reintroduce a strong centralized airborne organization. The years of scandal and scrutiny had taken their toll. On 12 April 1995 the plan for Canada's future airborne forces was announced. As expected, the news was disheartening.

Lieutenant-General Gordon Reay, the Commander of the Army, announced that the decision reached called for the maintenance of parachute-capable forces in Canada as a decentralized capability. "The Land Force," he explained, "will initially maintain its parachute capability by establishing three independent Parachute Company Groups reporting to their respective Brigade Headquarters. These independent Parachute Company Groups will be the lead elements of what will eventually be three Light Infantry Battalions, to be located at CFB Edmonton, Petawawa, and Valcartier."

The decision was disappointing but not surprising. Most had realized that the disbandment of the Canadian Airborne Regiment signalled the hiatus of the nation's airborne forces. In regard to military parachuting, the Army had simply reverted to a maintenance of capability mode. Brigadier-General Walter Holmes, the Director of Force Development at the time, candidly acknowledged that "we're just basically keeping the art alive."

As dispiriting as the outcome was for the airborne lobby within the Canadian Forces, there was an undis-

putable logic to the decision, captured eloquently by the SSF Commander at the time. "The present way ahead for the army's parachute capability," he wrote, "represents a 'minimum viable' approach which is seen to be consistent with both operational and financial realities. It permits basic levels of skill and expertise to be retained, but results in an extremely limited operational capability."

Time marches forward and waits for no man. By the the summer of 1995 a conscious purge of any vestiges of the past was undertaken. The Canadian Airborne Regiment logo was banned outright. Maroon quickly became a colour which attracted the censure and wrath of superiors in both CFBs Petawawa and Valcartier. The expurgation even extended to any type of maroon T-shirts. Senior military commanders seriously considered removing the distinctive maroon beret from the CF order of dress. Paratroopers realized that they, as well as the capability they represented, were once again being marginalized.

The summer of 1995 also marked the beginning of the end of 3 Commando Group. The annual posting season cut another swath through the ranks of the old cadre, taking with it the experience and corporate memory of the Canadian Airborne Regiment. The actual end came on 1 September 1995. On this date the Canadian Airborne Holding Unit ceased to exist and its personnel were absorbed by 3 RCR upon its move from CFB Borden to CFB Petawawa. Concomitant with this development was the transformation of 3 Commando Group into a new entity officially designated the RCR Parachute Company. It was now an integral sub-unit of 3 RCR, which in turn was one of the specified units chosen to become a light infantry battalion. The Canadian parachute capability returned to the Mobile Striking Force/Defence of Canada Force era.

Similarly, parachute activities took on a low priority both in the air force and in the units themselves. Rotations to Bosnia-Herzegovina and Haiti regularly crippled the availability and readiness of the contemporary Jump Companies. More importantly, parachute activity became dependent on the attitudes of the commanding cfficers of the light infantry battalions themselves, as well as their immediate superiors. One CO

Paratroopers preparing to enter the subterranean battle zone. *(Robert Prouse)*

Members of 8 Pl prepare to clear a building during FIBUA training. *(Robert Prouse)*

Cpl Thibodeau navigates through a jungle lane with a combat shotgun during a Cdo Gp live fire exercise in CFB Petawawa.
(*Robert Prouse*)

An RCR Para Company three-man reconnaissance patrol in CFB Petawawa.
(*Tony Balasevicius*)

Left and right: House entry drills.   *(Robert Prouse)*

bluntly acknowledged that "jumping is a real problem now." He stated that the Parachute Company, if lucky, will conduct a drop every three months. Moreover, he lamented, "we have went [sic] from an anything is possible, to an unsure, hesitant, 'maybe,' attitude."

The low priority the military is presently placing on parachute forces was further demonstrated in April 1999. At that time, the Army decided that it no longer required the maintenance of a battalion-level parachute capability. As a result, 159 jump positions were removed from the light infantry battalion establishments. Furthermore, the Canadian Parachute Centre was cut from eight annual basic parachutist course serials to six. Major-General Jeffries, the Deputy Chief of the Army, explained that "we made a pragmatic decision to economize in an area which is not a 'must-do' for us."

The fact was that the battalion capability had never been practised or even seriously considered since the establishment of the parachute companies. Jeffries candidly conceded, "it [parachuting] is desirable — desirable in terms of maintaining the capability, desirable from the soldier's point of view because of the extra challenge it provides. But we can't afford desirables." In the end the Army concluded that it had to "focus on the

'must-dos.'" The savings incurred by collapsing the "battalion" capability amounted to approximately $120,000.

The understandable degradation in airborne expertise inherent with the advent of a decentralized parachute capability, however, heightened the importance of the newly designated Canadian Parachute Centre (formerly known as the Canadian Airborne Centre), relocated to CFB Trenton in September 1996. The school now became instrumental as a focal point for all aspects of parachuting. In essence, it became a centre of excellence. All matters relating to parachute operations, standardization, and training now originate from this institution. Although severely limited in its actual influence on the respective parachute companies, the CPC's importance lies in its ability to perpetuate the skill and central doctrine of the airborne art and science.

In the end, the impact of all the events both before and after the defence minister's decision to decentralize the airborne forces indicates that the cycle had turned a full 360 degrees. The airborne was again marginalized. The Canadian paratrooper is once more operating in the shadow. As disappointing as this is to the airborne's supporters, it should not be a surprise. The absence of a credi-

Embarkation for a night drop.

(Tony Balasevicius)

ble role for paratroopers in Canada has always been their undoing. The "fire-brigade task," with the ability to rapidly project power, may be essential to some nations, but it has never been important to Canada. The nation's politicians have never shown a proclivity to dispatch troops on a moment's notice. There is a degree of wisdom in the "sober second look." To commit too quickly, or to possess the capability to become involved precipitously, can embroil a nation in events which in the dawn's light may be better ignored.

As a result, the nation's airborne soldiers have once again been relegated to their default position, namely the defence of Canada. But this requirement is tenuous as well.

Historically, intelligence assessments have consistently emphasized the reality that Canada faces no direct military threat. Alas, how much should a nation invest in a capability of questionable necessity? The decision at present is for the "minimum viable" capability. This represents the risk the government and the Department of National Defence are willing to accept based on the likelihood of tasks which may necessitate the exclusive employment of airborne troops. As such, the parachute companies, within their respective light infantry battalions, represent the nation's current airborne capability. Although a shadow of its former self, this capability ensures that the art, skill, and more importantly, the airborne spirit survive.

The RCR Para Company escape and evasion and jungle survival training during Ex Mainyard Garden, in Jamaica, February 1996.
(Tony Balasevicius)

An assault on Landry Crossing, CFB Petawawa, by the RCR Parachute Company, winter 1996. *(Tony Balasevicius)*

Ex Frozen Gun. *(Tony Balasevicius)*

Ex Frozen Gun. An RCR Parachute Company winter defensive position live fire exercise.
(Tony Balasevicius)

Top and above: The preservation of a capability. *(Tony Balasevicius)*

Parachute Company airmobile drills. *(Tony Balasevicius)*

Live fire FIBUA training in Fort Blanding, Florida, spring 1996. *(Tony Balasevicius)*

Cpls Chalmer and Nutter rig their equipment for the RCR Parachute Company's Ex First Step, in Earlton, Ontario, 1996. (*3 RCR*)

RCR Parachute Company airmobile operations during Ex Eastern Thunder, April 1997.   (3 RCR)

Top and above: Basic Parachutist Course candidates prepare for the Mock Tower.

(Greg Leclair, CPC)

The 34-foot "Tower of Terror." Despite its solid and stationary disposition, the Mock Tower provides a test of will for aspiring paratroopers. *(Greg Leclair, CPC)*

Faith in one's equipment.

(*Greg Leclair, CPC*)

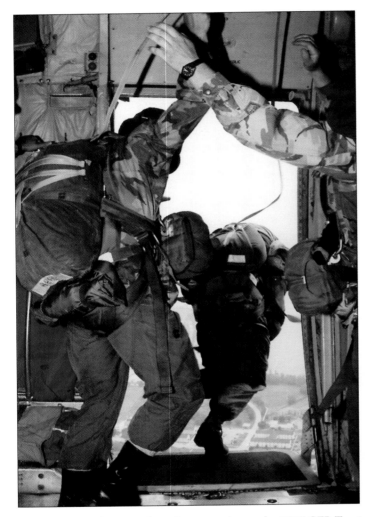

CPC staff provide a parachute demonstration at the 1998 CFB Trenton Airshow.

(CPC)

Heavy equipment drops and trials remain important missions for the CPC.

(Greg Leclair, CPC)

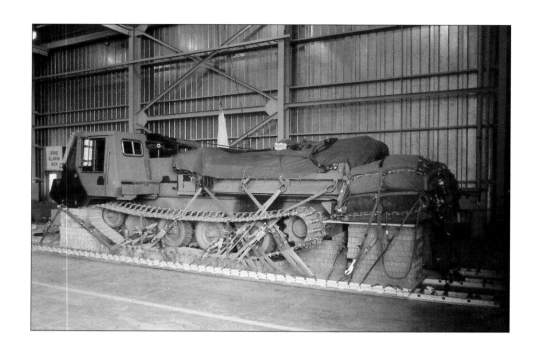

Top and above: A NODWEL all terrain vehicle and a LOSV rigged by CPC for a parachute drop.
(CPC)

Parachute company refresher aircraft drill. Due to the inherent elements of anxiety, fear, and stress when jumping, as well as the need for instantaneous reaction to a problem or potentially hazardous situation, parachuting drills and individual "IAs" (Immediate Action drills) must be instilled into the paratroopers so that all reaction is immediate and instinctive. *(3 RCR)*

Members of "A" (Parachute) Coy, 3 PPCLI load onto a US Army Chinook for a parachute descent onto DZ Saville Farm in Wainwright, Alberta, May 1999. *(3 PPCLI Archives)*

Pte Rogers from "A" (Parachute) Coy, 3 PPCLI assaults a trench during Ex Light Warrior, September 1998. *(3 PPCLI Archives)*

"A" (Parachute) Coy, 3 PPCLI receive an American JM brief during a Small Unit Exchange with the 2nd Bn, 75th Ranger Regiment, in Fort Lewis, Washington, March 1999. *(3 PPCLI Archives)*

MCpl White from "A" (Parachute) Coy, 3 PPCLI receives his American Jump Wings from a Ranger of the 2nd Bn, 75th Ranger Regiment, in Fort Lewis. *(3 PPCLI Archives)*

PART VI

CONCLUSION

n many ways, the Canadian airborne
experience is analogous to a roller-
coaster with its many peaks and valleys,
its gut-wrenching twists and turns. Yet, in the final analysis it has followed a very predictable cycle. In the absence of a pervasive role mer-
iting the investment of scarce resources, the innumerable airborne organizations have existed in a perpetual environment of peril. Proposals for
the downsizing and complete disbandment of the various parachute
units were perennially ambient. Budgetary pressures and fiscal restraints
persistently raised the question of affordability.

The 1994 White Paper signaled the most recent eclipse of our national airborne capability. The document's emphasis on generic multipur-
pose combat-capable forces, extenuated by the conspicuous absence of
any reference to airborne or parachute organizations or troops, cleared
the way for an eventual dismemberment of the last vestiges of Canada's
airborne structure. The assessment to collapse this capability can now
be taken without contradicting the existing government-mandated
defence policy. The effect of such a decision is difficult to project. The

issue of airborne forces, from their very inception, has always been emotionally charged. Paratroopers have invariably represented the best of the country's combat soldiers. They reflected a distinct warrior caste. They were widely recognized as the more adventurous, aggressive, motivated, physically fit, and tough soldiers in the Army. Their "can-do, anything is possible" attitude became a central tenet of their philosophy.

Their strength, however, was also their greatest weakness. The camaraderie forged in the furnace of shared hardship and hazard developed a tightly knit fraternity which welcomed fellow "jumpers" from all nations, but treated their non-airborne compatriots with an aloofness which invited enmity. This animosity often fueled the malevolent debate which invariably swirled around the question of the relevance of airborne forces.

Justifiably, the query, "why do we need airborne forces?" was routinely advanced. Certain realities have always existed. Regrettably for Canada's paratroopers, a high-readiness strategic unit required as a quick reaction force for national power projection has never been a crucial factor in Canadian thinking. To major powers such as Britain, France, Russia, and particularly the United States, the rapid deployment of military force is seen as a strength. Canadian politicians, however, see it as a potential liability. There is a degree of safety in delay. Undeniably, following a beaten path is less fraught with risk and far less onerous than breaking trail. Of equal importance, it also minimizes resource consumption. Alas, in the Canadian context, the DCO role was the only task which could ostensibly require a rapid-reaction parachute-insertion capability. But the risk of an internal security problem of such magnitude that it necessitated the drastic step of committing combat troops to a parachute assault was, and still remains, unlikely. In addition, technological advancement in aircraft, air-to-air refueling, as well as the proliferation of airfields throughout the North, makes alternate means of force entry plausible. In regards to the nebulous MAJAID role, Search and Rescue personnel, augmented if necessary by CPC staff, provide a legitimate response to this doubtful scenario.

Although sacrilege to airborne supporters, the reality is that Canada's airborne forces have never been required to perform a task that could not be, and was not, performed by more conventional units within the same time-frame. Operationally speaking, the absence of an airborne force would not seriously impact on the ability of the Canadian Forces to carry out its mandate.

Nevertheless, the debate is not so easily resolved. The relevance of a parachute capability is deeply rooted in the intangible benefits derived from training for airborne operations. It provides a challenge for those individuals who strive to test themselves and achieve a level of soldiering beyond that offered by the more conventional units. As such, the demanding and hazardous nature of airborne soldiering provides a "leadership nursery" effect which allows the experiences and skills developed to be cross-pollinated to the other units. It is also a vehicle for testing the courage, endurance, as well as mental and physical stamina of soldiers in a peacetime environment. This in fact was one of the very reasons General Jean Victor Allard argued so passionately for the establishment of a centralized airborne regiment in the mid sixties.

The existence of an airborne capability is also critical to the Army in regards to unity. The nation's parachute organizations have overwhelmingly encapsulated Canada's cultural mosaic, particularly in regard to anglophone and francophone personnel. This provided the vehicle to promote and enhance cultural awareness, as well as to establish personal ties which individuals would take back with them on return to their parent units. In short, it was a shared experience, a common bond, which united all those who answered the call to serve.

Finally, the existence of paratroopers allows the Canadian military to remain a member of the international/airborne fraternity. This provides for the continuing exchange of ideas and personnel with foreign airborne units and special operations forces. Although commonly dismissed as irrelevant, the long-term effects cannot be ignored. Membership to the "club" enhances links to applicable research and development, operational compatibility in coalition operations, and to professional contacts beneficial for future activities. Furthermore, it promotes goodwill and a sound partnership with the country's allies. Although exchanges between more conventional units continue to exist, Canada will become shut out in the realm of special

One constant throughout the Canadian Airborne experience has been the timeless and unconquerable spirit of the Canadian paratrooper. The following pages capture that intrepid, indomitable quality.

(CAFM)

operations forces. Significantly, this niche, within land forces world-wide, has seen the greatest growth and employment since the late eighties. Conversely, the absence of these links will eventually relegate the institution to an isolated military backwater of little interest or knowledge to other forces.

Clearly, the relevance of an airborne capability is not easily dismissed. Its demise would be a serious psycho-

logical and symbolic loss for the Army. Paradoxically, although often viewed as outcasts and pariahs, Canada's intrepid paratroopers have always represented the best combat soldiers this country has been able to offer. Renowned for their courage, initiative, physical prowess, and indomitable spirit, the nation's paratroopers have always represented the proficiency of the Canadian Army.

(Robert Prouse)

(Bernd Horn)

(1 Cdn Para Bn Assn)

(CAFM)

(Photographer unknown, NAC, PA169958)

246

(*CAFM*)

(Fraser Eadie)

(Eamonn Barry)

(3 RCR)

249

(Sgt Snashall, CFPU CNL, Neg. ISC 93-81)

251

(CFPU CNL, Neg. PAC 94 -35-33)

Left and right: The airborne spirit — metal and flesh.

(Don Halcrow and CAFM)

(Ken Bell, CFPU CNL, Neg. ZK-116)

(CAFM)

(CAFM)

GLOSSARY OF ABBREVIATIONS

AMF(L)	ACE [Allied Command Europe] Mobile Force (Land)
ARDC	Airborne Research and Development Centre
ASSU	Airborne Signals Support Unit
AVGP	Armoured Vehicle General Purpose
BOI	Board of Inquiry
BSP	Basic Security Plan
CABC	Canadian Airborne Centre
CAST	Canadian Air-Sea Transportable Brigade
Cdn AB Regt	Canadian Airborne Regiment
Cdn AB Regt BG	Canadian Airborne Regiment Battle Group
1 Cdn Para Bn	1st Canadian Parachute Battalion
2 Cdn Para Bn	2nd Canadian Parachute Battalion
CDS	Chief of the Defence Staff
CFS	Canadian Forces Station
CFB	Canadian Forces Base
CDHSR	Canadian Division Headquarters and Signals Regiment
Cdo	Commando
CFOO	Canadian Forces Organizational Order
CGS	Chief of the General Staff
CIBG	Canadian Infantry Brigade Group
CJATC	Canadian Joint Air Training Centre
CJFS HQ	Canadian Joint Forces Somalia Headquarters
CMBG	Canadian Mechanized Brigade Group
CMHQ	Canadian Military Headquarters
CFPU CNL	Canadian Forces Photographic Unit Central Negative Library
Coy	Company
CPC	Canadian Parachute Centre (formerly CABC)
CPTC	[A-35] Canadian Parachute Training Centre
CPTS	[S-14] Canadian Parachute Training School
C6	Current issue 7.62mm General Purpose Machine Gun
C7	Current issue 5.56mm Rifle
C9	Current issue 5.56mm Light Machine Gun
DCF	Defence of Canada Force
DCO	Defence of Canada Operations (or Deputy Commanding Officer)
DMZ	Demilitarized Zone
DND	Department of National Defence
DZ	Drop Zone
FMC	Force Mobile Command
FNC1(SLR)	Predecessor to the C7 - (7.62mm x 53 Self-Loading Rifle designed by Fabrique Nationale of Belgium)
FSSF	First Special Service Force
GPMG	General Purpose Machine Gun (7.62mm)
HALO	High Altitude Low Opening [military freefall parachuting]
HQ	Headquarters
HRS	Humanitarian Relief Sector [Somalia]
ICBM	Inter-Continental Ballistic Missile
JAS	Joint Air School
JM	Jumpmaster
L Edmn R	Loyal Edmonton Regiment
LFC	Land Force Command (formerly FMC)
LIB	Light Infantry Battalion
MAJAID	Major Air Disaster
MSF	Mobile Striking Force
NA	National Archives of Canada
NAC	National Archives of Canada (unofficial abbreviation)
NATO	North Atlantic Treaty Organization
NDHQ	National Defence Headquarters
NECIC	North European Command Infantry Competition [NATO]
NORAD	North American Air Defence (later Aerospace) Command
NRMA	National Resources Mobilization Act
OC	Officer Commanding (normally a company or commando)
P-Hour	Parachute Hour (time a drop will commence)
PI	Parachute Instructor
PIAT	Projector Infantry, anti-tank
PMW	[A-35] Parachute Maintenance Wing
PPCLI	Princess Patricia's Canadian Light Infantry
QOR of C	Queen's Own Rifles of Canada
R22eR	Royale 22ième Régiment/Royal 22nd Regiment
RCAF	Royal Canadian Air Force
RCE	Royal Canadian Engineers
RCIC	Royal Canadian Infantry Corps
RCR	Royal Canadian Regiment
R du Sag	Régiment du Saguenay
R Westmr R	Royal Westminster Regiment
SAS	Special Air Service
SF	Special Forces
SMG	Sub-machine gun (9mm)
SOF	Special Operations Forces
SSF	Special Service Force
UN	United Nations
UNAMIR	UN Assistance Mission in Rwanda
UNFICYP	UN Force in Cyprus
UNITAF	Unified Task Force (Somalia)
UNPROFOR	UN Protection Force (Former Yugoslavia)

INDEX